Hidden Goddess Revealed:
Book 1

D. Y. Robbins

Copyright © 2017 D. Y. Robbins

All rights reserved. No parts of this book may be copied or reproduced without permission of the author.

LEGAL DISCLAIMER

The author of this book shall not be held liable under any law of contract or tort for the contents or validity of statements herein. Though the author strives to ensure the accuracy of all information referenced, the biography may at times include inaccurate or subjective information, possibly based on the author's own experience/s, and therefore the accuracy of facts herein can in no way be guaranteed. Every effort has been made for personal details to be changed in accordance with the relevant Data Protection laws. All persons referenced in this book are strictly represented under the doctrine of fair use and educational purpose. Any resemblance to real persons, living or dead is purely coincidental. You must not copy, redistribute, sell, rent, lease, convey, or sublicense this book in any way. By purchasing or in any way accessing this book, you declare your unconditional understanding and compliance to the above and agree to hold harmless the author/s to the fullest degree allowed by law in all of its formats.

Hidden Goddess Revealed
Book 1

Author: D. Y. Robbins

E mail: HGR7711@gmail.com

Website: Hiddengoddessrevealed.com

Acknowledgements

Thanks to the Divine Mother for gracing us with her presence on Earth. Although many of us have been misled into forgetting you, we know deep down that you are within all of us. We are so grateful to be alive during this time of awakening and to be in the presence of your love.

Thanks to Spirit for guiding us together in our physical union.

A NOTE FROM DEE

For most of my life, I have hidden who I really am. I hid my true being in the shadows, and I hid so thoroughly that even I did not dare to look. It took the encouragement of my King for me to leave those shadows and share my story, first with him and now with the world.

Table of Contents

Preface 1

Dee: My Story 5

Visions from an Ancient Soul 11

Birth of the Divine Child 16

First Memories 18

Dee Speaks 20

The Mystery Schools 22

Blood Ritual: First Trip Abroad 25

Abuse and Retribution 27

The Mason Gathering 36

The Probing 37

Racist Cop 39

The Cabin and the Beach House 42

The Cabin: Struck by Lightning 46

The Cabin: Spider Bites 49

Group Healing 52

Solomon's Special Chair 54

Challenges: Red Balls 58

Challenges: Fire Walking 64

Challenges: Dangerous Town 68

Missing Son 71

Challenges: The Crystal Key and the Labyrinth 78

The Opera and the Cave Ritual 94

The Travel Agent 101

Egypt: The Funeral and the Pyramid Ritual 105

A Royal Call 115
Ancient Cave 123
Visiting Wild Animals: The Black Panther 138
Visiting Wild Animals: The Wolves 145
The Bell Ritual 154
Visiting Wild Animals: The Great Polar Bear 159
Submarine 171
Ancient Love Story: The 77 Revelation 176
Epilogue 181
Glossary 184

Preface

All that is hidden shall be revealed.

I am Vince. The information my wife and I have to share will require some readers to temporarily suspend their disbelief. Otherwise a significant story may be rejected.

My wife Dee was born in November of 1965. Her divine birth was prophesized by the Ancients, and she possessed vast supernatural powers and abilities. Dee also had daily dreams and visions of me since she was a child, and she used those abilities to find her way to me on September 1, 1985. She achieved this after years of searching and navigating the obstacles placed in her way. Dee finally found me when she was nineteen years old, and I had just turned twenty-three. I was immediately attracted to her peaceful nature and simple innocence. There was something else at my core gravitating me towards her, but I just didn't know what it was. Beyond her gentleness, I sensed that she had been deeply hurt and the scars still remained. She had two children when we met: a twenty-five-month-old girl and a seven-month-old boy. It didn't matter how many children she had, I just knew I loved her deeply and felt a connection to her like none that I had ever felt in my life. It was a depth of emotion that had eluded me until the moment I saw her. I knew this was the woman with whom I would spend the rest of my life. As it turns out, I was right, because we have been married for over thirty years.

Surprisingly, it has taken my wife twenty-nine of those years to share the secrets of her past with me. We were never religious, but in 2009 I began studying Buddhism and the mysteries of the occult.[1] My studies led me to practice various forms of meditation and breathing techniques which allowed me to open my mind and experience things beyond the physical world. I was amazed at the experiences I had and encouraged my wife to join me. I never knew how naturally gifted she was, and she never said a word. Then in 2012, we were able to cut a lot of negative people out of our lives, and I shared even more about my new spiritual discoveries. That's when she took the opportunity to tell me about a secret supernatural ability

---

[1] Occult: Hidden, secret. The term is sometimes taken to mean knowledge that is "meant only for certain people" or that "must be kept hidden."

she was born with: her ability to see and perceive things not visible to the senses. It can be referred to as a unique second sight. Everything is energy, and with her gift, Dee can see the essence of people, places, and things. That's one of the ways she ultimately found me. Another benefit her gift gives her is the ability to see microchip[2] implants in the human body. Dee has seen many people with microchips in their bodies, and many of them may not even be aware. I was amazed at her revelation, and we both became even more involved in our spiritual pursuits.

Two years later, on July 7, 2014, which was my 52nd birthday (7777), we had a breakthrough. We were meditating at our fireplace, a practice that had become a nightly ritual for us. A feeling came over me, and I began writing numbers that were coming through in my mind's eye. I started with 72, and other numbers followed. Next, I wrote birth dates I knew of, previous addresses where we had lived and phone numbers we had. In the process, I noticed some recurring numbers, such as my mother-in-law's frequent association with the number 33[3]. That number was her actual address, it was the day, month, and year of her birth, and later I discovered it was also included in many other numbers associated with her life. As I continued evaluating what I wrote down, I realized for the first time that most of the numbers associated with myself and my wife were essentially 11 and/or 77. They were showing up everywhere and were part of our last three addresses, and for the first time in my life, I began to pay attention. I had never studied numerology or number symbolism and hadn't given much consideration to my 7/7 birthdate. However, I recalled a photograph I once saw of my wife when she was just a child. It was one of the only pictures she had from her past, and she was wearing a number 77 sports jersey. I asked Dee about it, and she couldn't remember the photo, so I set out to find it.

I searched everywhere and finally found it. I showed Dee the photo, and she cried, as tears streamed down her face. In all our years together I can only remember my wife crying once, so I embraced her until she was ready to let me in on what was going on. "My father Solomon gave that shirt to me on my seventh birthday as a reminder to always use my gifts to look for you. I have been dreaming of you since I was a child!" she cried out.

---

[2] One purpose of micro chipping is to influence the thoughts and behaviors of humans without their knowledge and against their free will. Another is tracking.

[3] 33-A number revered by Freemasons, the Illuminati and occultists. A master number.

"My father was King Solomon in another life, and he had a vision of you on my seventh birthday. He and I called you the 77 Boy!"

The revelation caused us both to dissolve into tears of happiness. We always knew we were unique beings and were meant to be together. The photo was taken in Los Angeles years before she found me. Seeing the photo triggered the awakening of repressed memories of her childhood with her father, and her past began to emerge from the locked away corners of her mind.

Photo of Dee in 1979

Her life experiences were so incredible that I knew they had to be chronicled. So in late 2014, we began our journey into her past, complete with happy times, rituals, deceit, and even death. In the process of writing the story, we received visions of past lives that we have had together.

Who are we? We are love, and we are sharing our ancient love story replayed in modern times. Spirit has indeed blessed us, and through inner wisdom and desire for truth, we know this is our last physical presence on this Earth. We are so grateful to be together but all the same, we cherish our relative privacy and would much rather keep our private life out of public view, especially considering humanities doubting frame of mind.

Dee's story was publicly revealed because I was spiritually led to step out of my comfort zone and share her light with you. Dee is remarkably humble and has always been very reluctant to affirm her true self. Nonetheless, with her agreement, we created these books as a service to those who may resonate with them. We expect most to disbelieve what we have written, and this is what those who are aware of Dee's presence on Earth are counting on. In our observations, an overwhelming number of human beings are trapped in religious, political and social paradigms which are merely control mechanisms put in place by 'ruling forces' for mass consumption. Many secrets in the world are hidden from public view, and we are revealing a few in this modest book.

The memories that Dee has written about and that I have produced had been very challenging to set forth for several reasons. One is that some ruling forces don't want you to know or believe the truth. We also lacked the basic writing skills and budget necessary to produce it, and because we didn't personally know anyone that could help, we had to reach out to strangers. In the process of endeavoring to get professional assistance to express the highest vision of our story, we encountered obstacles as expected, but that has not deterred us from our mission to disclose.

The stories Dee wrote are part of a collection of memories about her life that she has recalled and agreed to share publicly. Since this book covered a time period when she was just a child under seven years old, it would be impossible to produce a comprehensive account of her experiences. As a child, Dee wasn't told very much because of her youth. When Dee writes about her past, she visualizes and relives them. As a result, she recalls the smallest details with accuracy. Some of those details we have truthfully included in this book.

The revelation of the living Ancient Mother on Earth, cloaked as a humble woman of color in America will be very hard to accept for most, and we are aware of that. The ruling forces have duped many people into forgetting the Ancient Mother. We're also mindful of the fact that a vast majority of the general public is not ready to accept this divine being on Earth in her present form. It's not our intention to substantiate or convince anyone of anything. We simply do not care what anyone believes. The book was written truthfully and to the best of our limited writing ability. Spirit is our only guide, and we are fully protected. Geb shall always surround Nut....... 7117

With that, I turn the attention back to Dee and her extraordinary life before birth to seven years old.

Dee: My Story

I never thought my life story was worth sharing with anyone, and certainly not worth writing a book about. I was tricked into believing that my past with my father Solomon should never be spoken about to anyone, especially my husband. I believed that for decades, even as we both were subjected to various rituals throughout our lives. I knew they were intrusions upon us, but I kept silent. I kept secrets as a result of the many years of deception I was subjected to after my father was killed in 1977. My King has never rejected me, and he has always been in my heart. The few people around us couldn't understand his love for me, as well as my deep love for him, but that never mattered to either of us.

I lived a very reclusive life, even though I was the youngest of eight children. I was different from my half-siblings in every conceivable way. I had a peaceful and innocent nature, whereas my half-siblings were the complete opposite. I was my father's only child with my mom, and the only child of hers to have their biological father involved in their life. Just as it was in the past, I still do not have any bonds with my mom's children. As a child, my life was very separate from theirs, which turned out to be for a good reason. I was rejected, teased, tricked and sometimes abused by them. They knew I was different, but they didn't know the extent of it. I had a false notion that they were family, and that belief left an opening for them to trick me at will, even as I became an adult. Once all this negative contact was severed, I was able to focus more on what was real to me, without any interference from outsiders. This was one of the keys that got me past the preconceived notions I had established about keeping secrets. Their actions toward me throughout my life did not penetrate my being, and I have never held any anger toward my mom's children.

I was born with supernatural powers and abilities, but as a child, I did not yet know how to fully control my gifts. That was a mission my father set out to help me accomplish by making sure I attended the secret mystery schools he knew about. One of the abilities I had was a high tolerance for pain. I had to learn over time what pain meant to a human and how it felt. My half-siblings witnessed me get hurt a few times and saw that I had a minimal reaction. That awareness was used as an excuse to abuse me at times, and sometimes I retaliated. One of the ways I retaliated was to make them sleep uneasily by entering into their dreams (which is one of the abilities I have always had). When I was young, I used that ability as a means of self-defense; by entering into their dreams I thought they would stop their badgering. Merely making my presence known while they slept would give them a glimpse of the kind of powers I yielded. It worked for a while, but my youth and innocence caused them to overcome their cautiousness, and soon their cruel games began anew. I did not use my abilities to protect myself very often because Mom would scold me when I did. She would always tell me that I could hurt them much more than they could hurt me. Although that was true, my objective was to stop their cruel treatment, not to hurt them. My mom had been taught to fear my supernatural powers and was intent on suppressing me. Nevertheless, on occasion, she would ask me to use my abilities to help her sleep. She liked the benefit of that ability, and since I was capable of helping her, I did.

Our home did not offer me much privacy, and I was always careful not to let others see me use my gifts. I knew that if my half-siblings found out about some of the other abilities I possessed, they might try to use that information against me. I did manage to teach myself to levitate my physical body, but rarely found an occasion to practice in my room without being caught. As a one-year-old child, my dad would take me with him to his hunting cabin. While at the cabin and with his encouragement, I was able to practice levitation more freely. Even so, he told me to stay aware that 'they' were always watching us wherever we went. I was able to understand and say words as a baby, and I assured my dad that there were eyes on us. Perhaps we were sensing remote viewers, but who knows.

I also honed my second sight[4] while at my dad's hunting cabin. One of my unique attributes is the ability to see beyond the physical world. To see people, places, and things as they really are: energy. As a baby, I remember my second sight turning on and off uncontrollably until I learned how to use it at will. I thought everyone had a second sight and saw the same things as I did. I realized that wasn't the case after talking with my father about it. He told me that the sight was my special gift and mine alone and that I was not like any other child.

---

[4] Second sight, or extrasensory perception, is the ability to detect and receive information that is invisible to standard human senses.

I would use any chance I could to escape the house when my father left me alone with my mom and half-siblings. I didn't like being there without him because of the badgering I would receive. One way I escaped was through my ability to astral travel[5] at will. This gift allowed me to flee humanity and travel in spirit whenever I wanted. I expanded my consciousness and gained an astral body separate from my earthbound physical body. I still do this at will to this day. I would often take long naps and travel out of my body when my father left me at home. No one disturbed me because if they did, I would tell on them and my dad would scold them every time.

During my out-of-body travels, my second sight allowed me to see the planet's energy. I am capable of adjusting the energy of the planet, and I often do, making it smoother and more positive. It is impossible for me to explain it any better, but my father could feel the changes I made. He would commend me and advise me to continue to do it. I have been making needed adjustments to the Earth's energy ever since I was a child, without wanting or receiving any attention or acknowledgment from anyone.

With every journey into the spirit world, it became harder for me to return to the physical Earth. The spirit world has always been my playground. I was loved, powerful, free and sometimes even needed. At home, I was subjected to ridicule, trickery, and cruelty at the hands of my mom and half-siblings. I always felt that I should have been isolated from those who looked at me with coldness in their hearts whoever they were. That I should have been protected and honored. There always remained a shred of hope that this physical life was all just a test—one that I would have to master—and after which all would be over. This proved to be true when I searched for and finally found my soul mate and King many years later, and happiness prevailed. Nevertheless, until I found him, my father was the only anchor tying me to the physical world. I toyed with the idea of staying out of my body many times, yet my father's energy always pulled me back to Earth. Knowing that I would see him again kept me from letting my body die. Had I chosen to stay out-of-body permanently, I would have eventually been left with no earthly vessel in which to return. My father made life on Earth worth living for me, and I was happy with him.

---

[5] Astral projection, or astral travel, is the act of leaving one's own body as a soul, spirit, etc., and entering a spiritual realm normally inaccessible to the living.

My father Solomon was an amazing man, shrouded in more mystery than I. In a previous life, he was King Solomon, an archetype of Osiris, and he was of a royal bloodline even in this life. He had relatives in Egypt who were of a royal family. Agencies, Freemason leaders and influential people around the world secretly heralded him as a very significant person. Appearances were important to Solomon, and he was hardly ever seen wearing anything other than a business suit. He worked with influential people and was able to amaze them with his prophecies and impressive skill with numbers. He too had abilities, and would sometimes use them to help people become wealthy and successful. My father had been married once before meeting my mom and had three sons with his previous wife. However, he called me his only 'divine child,' the child foretold to come to Earth by the Ancients. Solomon possessed the gift of foresight and knew who the mother of the child would be years before they actually met.

`I was the magician as a child and was in my most powerful state[6]. I felt that I could carry out miraculous feats, especially with the right training and guidance. This is why my father wanted me to attend the secret mystery schools. However, he was murdered in 1977 when I was 11 years old, (7711), an unfortunate, tragic event that changed my life completely. I was targeted for suppression—thus temporarily putting an end to my rise. Without the intrusion upon my physical life, I was to be a beacon of truth and light for those who may be lost in this temporary world. The ruling forces did not accept me in my physical form and began a covert war to suppress my divine powers and memory.

My mom Ella was instrumental in their plans because she was the only person I had to rely on in life. By using my second sight, I could see that she been implanted with microchips[7] throughout her body. I had seen the devices in so many people and never knew what they were until Vince

---

[6]Magic is not tricks or illusion. Magic of the Ancient world is a spiritual, scientific aspect of manipulating the laws of the universe, and the elemental spirits around you. It's the highest form of magic.

[7]Microchip - technological devices that can be implanted directly into a person's brain. Such an implant creates an interactive link between the human brain and supercomputers. One purpose of micro chipping is to influence the thoughts and behaviors of humans without their knowledge and against their free will. The implanted individual can be monitored and controlled from anywhere on the globe via satellites. Brain function can be remotely altered through the changing of frequencies. Microchips are manufactured from silicon, and once implanted, are almost impossible to detect without specialized equipment and trained personnel. Also used for tracking and identification.

brought me some photos and research on the subject of microchip implants. When I saw the pictures, I knew that they were the devices I had been seeing inside the bodies of so many people. I then began recalling several instances of micro-chipped individuals displaying strange behavior around me and claiming not to remember when they were questioned about it. Or they would say, "I don't know why I acted that way." Although it's said that microchips are used for tracking and identification, from our experience we know that some are used for much more than that. The implants in my mom were one of the ways they kept control over her, and why she became fixated on suppressing me. I could never blame her, but our relationship has been severed because of her conditioning and deeds. My mom, Ella, claims that she doesn't remember any of the past and lives in denial to this day. However, she has come to me in private several times crying out and apologizing for what she had done. Those moments of realization were very brief, and she would soon claim to forget again.

My father left me with vast financial wealth when he passed away. It was enough for me to remove myself from wherever I didn't want to be and live a very comfortable life. The inheritances were my lifeline in case the other preparations he made for me failed. All of what he had prepared was taken away. The final suppression of my wealth was the taking of my inheritance, a solid gold chest similar to the one on the cover of this book. A few of the items inside the chest were my father's journal, a wax-sealed letter to the '77 Man,' and many pouches filled with marble-sized precious gems, some of which I saw my father receive during a trip to Egypt. The act of suppressing my great wealth had little effect on me because I always knew my true essence was far greater than any temporary prosperity on Earth. It's just how I've always been, and many have taken advantage of that lack of importance I have concerning material wealth. Nonetheless, my King and I among many others would have had entirely different physical lives without the intrusion and thievery of the 'ruling forces.'

You might ask who my King is. I have had daily dreams and visions of Vince my entire life. He was always a little taller and a little older than I. The first time I physically saw him was as a baby, and I left my body and traveled to his home. It just suddenly happened one day, and I found myself in his room and saw him playing with a race car set. I touched him, and afterward, he closed his eyes and smiled, but he could not see me. I soon left, and following that encounter, all my contact with him was in the spirit world. That's where we would share our gifts and marvel at each other's powers, as we built other worlds and explored them together.

Vince and I were happy, and as much as I wished to stay with him in the spirit world, my father on Earth overpowered those urges. Aside from my father and Vince, very few people ever treated me fairly. I was often taken advantage of throughout my life because of my innocent and trusting nature; I always thought the best of everyone. Interestingly, when those who failed to treat me fairly came to their ultimate end, every single one of them sought me out in spirit to beg for my help. I would like to say that I have helped everyone, but that would be false. I have helped very few reach their destination in the afterlife, as this is also a great ability that I possess. I believe this gateway is the ultimate eternal gift anyone could hope to receive and far beyond any temporary riches or status one may have on Earth.

This is my life, and I have chosen to share some of my memories with you through Vince. I am most comfortable telling my story in this manner and would have it no other way. The only light I share publicly is my story.

Visions from an Ancient Soul

Besides Dee just knowing, it took many out-of-body travels for her to fully realize that she is the Ancient Mother and the Soul of the Universe. She has been called this at various times throughout her life, but her natural essence has always kept her very humble. Although she considers her dreams and visions private, she has graciously agreed to share a few of her spiritual travels and visions with you here.

The Mother

Dee frequently visits otherworldly dimensions, and in this particular one, she was in the middle of a circle with the energies of humans surrounding her. The energies closest to her in the first circle had the greatest love for her, and there were many others lined up behind them as far as could be seen. They were all connected to each other, similar to a bloodline.

Dee was aware that she was the Mother, and they were feeding on her light. There were so many energies that it seemed as if every human being on the planet were surrounding her. She noticed that some of the energies lined up in the second concentric circle were not connected to her or to the others. They were skipped beings, and energy did not surround them as it did the others. Those skipped beings had deficient energy levels and were feeding off the others, not Dee. The ones connected to Dee had a great love for her, even if it had been buried deep inside. The skipped ones had no love for Dee, not even deep down.

Dee would often spend time in that place during her travels out of her body. Dee believes that the beings connected to her encompass all humanity, and the skipped beings not connected to her are presently ruling the Earth.

Protector of the Earth

During another one of her travels as a very young child, Dee unexpectedly left her body while sitting on a couch at home drawing in her book. It was as if she was needed in an instant and called upon by the spirit world. She suddenly came across a group of beings she had never seen before. She curiously approached them without fear. As she got closer, she realized they were draining the Earth and harming the planet. As a guardian of Earth, Dee asked them to stop, but they ignored her and continued. She repeated her demand, but once again she was ignored. She gave a final warning that she would have to stop them, but like so many before and after them, her powers were underestimated. In an instant, it became clear that the beings were incapable of love and were intent on harming Earth. They were leeching off its resources like a swarm of locusts, stripping the planet of its valuable energy. Dee could sense their history of harming and destroying other planets, so she had no other choice but to stop them.

They attacked her and were subsequently destroyed. In destroying them, their entire species was annihilated, and she felt it as soon as it happened. Despite their evil agenda, Dee had not intended to destroy all of them. However, before returning to her physical body, she realized that she had done what was necessary to protect Earth. Upon completely returning to her body, she became acutely aware that she had done something heroic. Dee told her dad about her experience, and he said, "As a protector of the planet you did what had to be done, and you can do no wrong."

Geb and Nut

The following is a vision that was received by Dee in early 2016. It is believed to be the story of our physical beginnings. It's a significant revelation meant for anyone who may resonate with it.

In the beginning, there were two forms of energy: Geb was the darkness and Nut was the light. They merged their energies together, an action which caused several huge explosions in the darkness. The darkness became a vast open space, and the light became all the stars. Some of the stars exploded and became suns. The darkness kissed one of the suns, causing another explosion to occur, and celestial bodies of planets filled the darkness of space. Shimmering rays of blue, red and gold energy merged with the dark energy, amalgamating into a combination of light and dark. The energies settled into the core of one of the newly formed planets now called Earth. They merged yet again, this time creating beings. The beings were shaped like humans (male and female) and their brains were all linked, allowing them to communicate instantly. Their bodies were almost transparent, and they radiated a glowing blue color, but still contained both light and dark energies within them.

The newly created beings created children of their own, and they lived in the core of the Earth for a very long time. They were the first to inhabit the planet, and the children that were created dwelled inside. They were very advanced, and as children could use a significant portion of their brainpower. Nut, the light energy, dwelled inside the female child of an original, while Geb, the dark energy, dwelled inside the male child of an original. Together, they lived as children for a very long time. During resting rituals and gatherings, their minds were not only linked but also synchronized. They could not feel or experience emotion as a modern human would today.

After many generations of living in the core of the Earth, Geb, who was still a child, wanted to explore feelings. He wanted to know how it felt to touch the surface or to feel his body. Geb's desires were manifested one day, and the next time his people rested their bodies, they miraculously evolved into beings that were more physical. They were no longer completely transparent, but they still glowed blue. This caused quite a stir among the people, as they were now experiencing their limited new senses and emotions. Nevertheless, Geb wanted to know and feel more. He wanted to explore the surface of the Earth. An elder warned Geb not to go to the surface, but he was disregarded. Geb planned to break his link to his people during the next resting ritual so he could explore the surface.

The resting ritual began every three days and would last a full turn of the Earth. The originals among the people were the first to be created in semi-physical forms. Those elders would lead the others to the very center of the Earth's core to begin the ritual. Within the core was an active volcano saturated with many layers of blackness inside. Lava flowed to the top of the volcano, spewing a stream of glowing blue magma onto the layers of shiny black rock. The blackness from deep inside the volcano gave way to the blue lava. The beings would drink the blue lava when the resting ritual began. As blue magma flowed from the volcano and onto the black surface, an impression that resembled a huge tree was formed. A branch from that tree went to the top and inside the volcano.

The tree was most sacred to the people and connected directly to them. Geb was the father and Nut, the mother. The originals would lay their bodies on the black surface, and around the impression of the tree. Others would gather around them, with the oldest beings closest to the originals and the youngest farther away. They rested their bodies until the Earth made a complete rotation. During the rest, merged light and dark energy flowed out of the beings and into the grooves of the sacred tree. The liquefied energies flowed to the single branch that reached the top of the volcano and continued inside until reaching the mass of blackness at the bottom. Then a burst of light and dark energies exploded into the universe. Nut is the light, and Geb the dark. Nut hovered over Geb, watching the universe they had created. Nut was the soul of her people; Geb was the spirit of his people.

One day the male child in whom Geb dwelled decided not to rest his body during the ritual. He was able to break the link with his people and venture to the Earth's surface. Once there, his body began to do things that it had never done before, such as take a breath, hear sounds and feel more sensations. He thought about Nut and his people in the core of the Earth and wanted them to experience the same new senses on the surface as he did. He left the surface to go back to the Earth's core before his people had completed their resting ritual. He tried to rush but lacked the energy needed for the journey, so he rested his body for a while before going further. It was the first time Geb had felt the sensation of being tired. He eventually reached the originals well after the Earth's full cycle and shared the news. They surrounded him and communicated with their minds, but before Geb could relay anything, he was interrupted. The originals were collectively disappointed by Geb's decision not to partake in the resting ritual.

An elder who knew of everything he'd experienced on the surface was well aware of the consequences of his actions. "Geb, you broke a branch of the tree, thus breaking the people's connection to the energy that flowed from the core of the Earth. As a result, the resting ritual was incomplete without you, and our bodies are not well rested. By continuing to go to the surface, you will eventually break your link to your people and lose your memory and power. The branch you broke may not be able to heal." Geb disagreed, but he didn't want the link to his people severed. Yet he wanted to seek answers that were beyond his people's ways. "This is our way and has been since the beginning," said an elder.

Another original female, who was the mother of the child in which Nut dwelled, spoke to Geb's mind. "You will definitely lose your connection to us if you go back to the surface and you may never find your way back." She continued, "Every time you experience emotion or do something new with your physical body, you will lose power and energy from your brain.

Eventually, you will forget who you and your people are, and you will be lost."

An elder who was a healer spoke to Geb's mind. "All our people could come together to heal the broken branch, but you must keep true to our ways and never venture to the surface again." Geb pondered this for a while and decided to speak to the mind of Nut, who dwelled in the body of a young female. Geb told her of his venture to the surface and what he had experienced. The things Geb said captivated Nut. She was older than Geb and knew of his desire to explore. She wanted to join him if he ever returned to the Earth's surface, regardless of the warnings given by the elders. So they both agreed to go before the originals to inform them of their wish to explore the surface.

Nut stood before the originals first and communicated her wish to go to the surface with Geb. They all relayed a message to her in unison. "If you go to the surface with Geb, we will suffer a break at the very root of the sacred tree. This will be the beginning of the end for our people. We cannot repair the root without the light of Nut's energy. We tell you once again that you will lose your connection with yourself and your people and you will lose energy. If you choose to dwell on the surface for long, it will change you, and you will only have a small percentage of energy left."

The originals were unable to convince either Geb or Nut to stay in the core of the Earth. Their desire to explore the surface was too strong to deny, and the elders knew that Geb and Nut were destined to be together. Wherever Geb went, Nut would eventually follow, and vice versa. So a special ceremony was arranged for them before they departed for the Earth's surface.

After making it to the surface, they began to forget about their people in the Earth's core. With every breath, a percentage of their brainpower was lost. With every new physical experience, more of their energy slipped away, until they were both down to possessing a minimal amount of their previous power. The new senses were incredible, but their beginnings were lost as they experienced more and more of the physical world. Sleeping was the only way they were able to energize and rejuvenate themselves. They lived happily in their new physical bodies and created the life that eventually evolved into the human beings we know of today.

Birth of the Divine Child

Dee was born in November of 1965. Her mom Ella was thirty-two years old and her dad Solomon was fifty-five. She was the child that Solomon had patiently waited for over the years. "Little D," as her dad would call her, was the divine child whose coming was prophesized in his visions. A child sent to Earth by the Ancients, possessing divine supernatural powers and vast abilities. Solomon knew that such a child should be raised with the utmost care and dedication.

Solomon had the gift of foresight and knew of his future wife many years before he actually met her. His eventual wife, Ella, was a slim, dark-skinned woman from a small southern town. It was difficult for Solomon to approach Ella because she was either pregnant or in a relationship. Ella was completely unaware of the negative forces that infiltrated and controlled her life. By the time Solomon was able to approach her, his wife to be had already given birth to seven children. He knew there were forces at work that had been preventing them from getting together and creating the divine child. If the objective of the forces was to make Ella less desirable to him because of her seven children, they clearly underestimated Solomon's resolve.

One day while Solomon was at a train station observing Ella, as he had done many times before, his opportunity finally presented itself. Ella was holding her youngest child Emma in her arms, and her son Fred was standing next to her. Both her children were under three at the time, and the father of her two youngest children was with her. He was intoxicated and badgered her for money. She continually refused to give him any, which only served to anger him. In a fit, he knocked his son down to the pavement hard, causing the boy's arm to break. Fred screamed out loud in pain as bystanders looked on, not lifting a finger to help either Ella or the child.

Solomon was outraged at the man's behavior. The father continued badgering Ella, even as she was helping her crying son. Solomon approached and grabbed the man from behind, throwing him to the ground. The man's arm broke in the fall, just as his young son's had a minute earlier. As he staggered away, Solomon shouted after him, "How do you like having your arm broken!" Solomon took Ella and her children to the nearest hospital and waited with her as her son's arm was being taken care of.

He looked into her eyes and asked, "What would you have done had I not intervened?" Ella sighed, clearly defeated, and responded, "What could I do? He's a mean bully, just as most of the men in my life have been." Solomon believed her, as he had witnessed how poorly other men had treated her in the past. The father of Ella's oldest daughter Betty was a biracial man that was nearly seven feet tall. They were a very odd-looking couple, as Ella was thin, short and dark. The man had no problem publicly displaying his disregard for the mother of his child as Solomon observed. He wanted to approach them, but the man was so crazy, he would have had to kill him to do it. So instead, he watched her from a distance and bided his time.

Solomon and Ella continued their conversation until Fred was treated, and that day marked the beginning of their relationship. They were married on October 29, 1965 (33). About a month before Dee's birth, and a year after they met. Despite the ongoing attempts by forces to delay the inevitable union. At the time the child's birth certificate was obtained, there were some questions about Solomon's true age. Solomon was born October 10, 1910, at 10 p.m., but on the records, his birth date had been registered as October 27, 1907, (77). He explained to Ella that *"they"* had altered his records and could do so with anyone's records if they so desired.

Unlike Solomon, Ella had not traveled. She had been raised as a small town country girl and had lived a relatively simple life, only having the chance to attend school until the fourth grade. Her mother had died during her birth, and her aunt had taken over raising her. For a very long time, Ella had been the victim of deception and trauma-based rituals.

Dee never blamed her mom for any wrongdoings she committed against her, of which there are many. It was never her fault; it was the fault of those that controlled her for years. Her mom had had no one to confide in since the moment she was born, whereas Dee at least had her father in her early life.

First Memories

Not only does Dee remember her birth, but she also clearly remembers[8] the sensations she felt in her body while she was in the uterus. She describes it as a feeling of floating in darkness, feeling calm and bliss at the same time. At birth, that feeling was suddenly interrupted by the sound of thunder. That sensation caused a shock to her infant system, which in turn caused a continuous motion in her lower back, and she became aware of being hungry for the first time. Then she felt matter being forced through her body, and soon after she heard voices outside the womb and felt herself expanding and growing.

She also remembers visits to a Shaman. Given the magickal nature of the unborn child, Solomon thought it would be better to take Ella to a Shaman he knew who lived deep in the bayou of Louisiana, rather than to any of the usual antenatal health providers. The Shaman was a tall, dark-skinned man with a long gray beard. The journey to his home included a car ride, a boat trip through the swamps and finally a walk through the woods.

While in her mom's uterus, Dee remembers one particular visit to the Shaman when he prepared an elixir to rub on her mom's stomach, explaining that it would allow him to hear the baby. It was at this point that Dee began to understand the words being spoken outside of the womb. She heard the Shaman give her mom instructions not to eat pork. Dee sensed the surprise her mom felt when the Shaman revealed that he knew about her eating habits. Regardless, she did not heed his words and continued her usual pork diet. The pork made Dee sick, as some parts of the meat's chemistry would infiltrate the placenta. When Dee was three years old, she told her dad of her memory while in the uterus. He was amazed. He gave her a hug and encouraged her to talk more about her experience.

---

[8] Research has shown that our first cognitive memories usually occur between the ages of three to four. These early memories are lost with age and are replaced with memories that are more current. This is referred to as "childhood amnesia." While we do have the capacity to remember events that occurred at age one and younger, most of us lose these memories as adults (Tustin and Hayne.) While there is not a lot of material available to support the idea that we have the capacity to remember our own births, *The Guardian* has asked the question, "Is it possible to remember being born?" (Guardian News and Media Limited. The responses were, for the most part, in line with the above research; however, at least 3% of the responders reported memories of their births.

Not long after she was born, Dee began to pay close attention to the sounds around her. She gravitated toward her dad's deeper voice because it was more soothing to her than that of her mom's higher pitch. After her birth, Solomon held her and said, "I'm Dad." That's when she put her tiny hands on his face and was able to feel his energy for the first time.

After giving birth, Ella was doing well, so they left the hospital right away which is what her dad wanted. The doctor wanted to keep Dee for a few more days, but Solomon absolutely refused. The nurse explained that the child needed some shots and Solomon refused again. As he loaded his family into the car, a hospital employee approached him in the parking lot to explain how the shots were required immunizations needed to prevent illness. He still refused and proceeded to drive away.

During the drive home, Solomon asked Ella why she had gone to the hospital to have the child instead of waiting for the midwives and Shaman he had arranged. Ella said she felt the baby was coming too quickly and she didn't want to wait. Once at home, Dee felt hungry and heard gurgling sounds in her stomach. Her mom fed her at her dad's request, and soon Dee fell asleep. She awoke sometime later to the feeling of warm water on her skin. She opened her eyes and saw her mom bathing her.

Dee Speaks

Dee remembers her dad taking her to the beach when she was a baby. He carried her out to the edge of the water and looked up to the sky. Then he presented her to the ancestors by lifting her up high in the air and saying some words. Solomon brought her back down and poured water from the ocean onto her forehead. He held her in front of him and smiled. In an instant, her face began to feel warm and tingly, and Dee spoke for the first time. Her dad was shocked, but Dee doesn't recall what was said. She does recall what he told her not to forget. He told her to never speak in front of others because they would not understand how a baby so young could speak and understand words. So she waited until she was older before speaking in the presence of anyone other than her dad.

Dee would often crawl on the floor trying to remove her diapers; she was just too advanced and didn't like wearing them. As a tiny baby, she would also try to stand and walk like the adults she saw. Her father would watch and laugh. "Your tiny legs are not yet strong enough to stand and walk like older people," he explained. Her dad frequently took her to his hunting cabin so they could have more privacy. There she could be free to do as she pleased without anyone around watching. He purchased small underwear for her and made a small commode in the cabin that she could use. They would spend hours in front of the fireplace, or he would carry her through the woods on long walks.

They arrived home late one night after a trip to the cabin, and her dad put her right to bed. Before he left her room, he put her diaper back on so nobody would know how advanced she really was. It wasn't long before Dee somehow climbed from her bed and managed to pull her diaper off. She left it in the hall and climbed onto the commode. Afterward, Dee crawled to a basket in her room and put on the underwear her dad had let her wear at the cabin. When her mom came into the room the next morning, she saw that the baby had underwear on. She yelled out to Solomon, forgetting that he'd left early for a meeting.

When Solomon returned later that day, Ella was watching television. Dee was in a high chair and was very hungry, but her mom wasn't paying attention to her. So she had to take matters into her own hands. Dee never cried like the other children. Whenever she was hungry, or something was wrong, she would patiently wait for the problem to be fixed. At only a few months old, Dee thought she was old enough to let her mom know what she wanted.

Dee made a noise to get her mom's attention. When her mom looked at her, she pointed to the kitchen and said, "Milk." She only drank the breast milk her mom would save for her. Ella was shocked as if she couldn't believe she'd just heard the baby speak. Again, Dee pointed to the kitchen and said, "Milk." Ella was floored. She backed away, knocking over and breaking a glass that was on the table. Solomon was in his room and came running when he heard the noise.

"Ella, what's wrong?" he asked.

"The child just spoke," Ella replied.

"I know," Solomon said.

"How long has she been speaking?" Ella asked.

"Quite a while now," he replied.

"It's too early. Dee is just a baby. It's way too early. I have to tell someone," said his wife.

Ella went right to the phone to inform someone about Dee. She told those that had been controlling her everything that occurred in the home. Solomon advised Ella against telling them every single thing that was going on with Dee, but she did it anyway, and there was nothing he could do about it.

During further talks with his young daughter, he asked, "How did you know that I was your dad when you were born?"

"I touched your face, and you said you were Dad," she replied.

"Do you know what it means to die?" he asked. No matter how strange this question was, Solomon asked it.

She shook her head to indicate no. He explained that he was old and would not be around for much longer and that one day his body would not be alive. Dee understood. "Yes, I see you will die first," she said. Solomon was surprised by her quick revelation. He told her there was work to be done to guarantee her entrance into the mystery schools where she could learn more about herself and her abilities.

The Mystery Schools

Solomon, in his age-old wisdom, knew about children with powers and abilities[9] long before any studies were conducted outside of government facilities. He was also aware of special hidden mystery schools that had been around for thousands of years. As such, he wanted Dee to attend the schools designed for individuals with special gifts. There are **6** schools located in **6** different countries worldwide. To the best of Dee's recollection, the schools are located in Africa, Russia, China, France, Greenland and a small Latin country. The schools are in remote areas for secrecy and exclusivity. To receive an invitation to the school, Dee was required to prove her worthiness. To Dee's knowledge, there are only **6** invitations awarded each year, and, once accepted, the students attend each of the **6** schools for **6** months each over **6** years.

It was critical for Solomon that she study at the mystery schools. He was aware that they could potentially learn even more from her than she would from them, but above all else, it was a safe place for her to grow into herself. He worked hard developing contacts and doing what was necessary to ensure that she would receive an invitation when the time was right. This was the main reason for most of their eventual travels, as Dee was destined to be a major force for good in the world. If just left alone, she would have shone her light onto the world as a shield to protect it and its inhabitants against the unseen evil forces that rule Earth. For her to reach her full human potential, training and guidance were necessary. The special schools were the holders of ancient hidden knowledge unavailable anywhere else. They would be instrumental in helping her discover herself, achieve mastery of her abilities, determine her position in the world and be of service at an even higher, more prominent level. The training would also keep entities determined to undermine her development from deceiving and manipulating her, as they had done with her mom.

---

[9] An increasing number of children are born with super psychic abilities every year. They exhibit such traits as "X-ray" vision, the ability to move objects through the air, and even to know the future. They are able to move solid objects through solid materials, read balls of paper placed in their ears, bend spoons solely through intention, and levitate as well. Drunvalo Melchizedek, in a 2011 article, stated that, "If these children don't change our world, nothing will." The Dream Magazine, a renowned scientific publication, further states, "These innocent children are demonstrating natural spiritual abilities that are relegated by most people to the realms of fantasy and movie special effects."

Dee and her dad traveled the globe in pursuit of their goals. She participated in testing rituals required by Freemasons and others to prove her "worthiness" to receive an invitation. Most of the participants undergoing testing were at least young adults, but it didn't matter, as Dee was unchallenged by her competition and passed all the tests that the adults could not.

At five or six years old, Solomon took her to a mystery school in the US. It was not one of the prestigious six schools, yet it was sanctioned by Freemasons, and they taught substantial magickal techniques. A Freemason leader had given special permission for Dee to attend. The school was located in what appeared to be an abandoned old college campus. On the grounds there stood a statue of a man holding one hand on his heart exposing all his fingers, and the other hand with one finger pointed upward. The statue was surrounded by three circles, the first of which was a marble surface, the second a grass surface and the third a concrete walkway. There were also three benches placed around the last concrete circle.

Solomon took Dee to the classroom and instructed her to have a seat inside. "I will be right outside the door in the hallway," he said. Once inside, Dee saw that twenty college-age white male students occupied the classroom, and she became the immediate focus of their attention. They whispered to each other and soon began voicing angry objections to her presence in the class. The teacher tried to calm them by explaining that she'd been given special permission to attend, but this did little to assuage their anger. They continued their complaints and advised that they would be informing their parents of the intrusion.

After hearing all the commotion, Solomon decided to enter the classroom and took a seat next to Dee. She noticed that the students possessed certain magick skills and were directing a very negative energy toward her dad. She quickly cleansed her father of the intrusive energy and the two of them left. Cheers from the students accompanied their exit. Solomon said, "Those students are rude, spoiled and not deserving of their position. Most likely they're the children of high-ranking Freemasons. We will never return." He assured her that when they returned home, he would be having a conversation with the leader that had given them special permission to attend the school.

Dee clearly remembers that her dad was always her champion. He accompanied her everywhere and paved the way for her safety and acceptance in the mystery schools. It's sad to note that these schools are hidden from the public eye, and controlled by Freemasons, who also held the keys to Dee's admission. Solomon and Dee were required to do "favors" for various affiliations, agencies and sometimes even mobsters with ties to Freemasonry. Solomon did what was necessary for the benefit of his special child.

On a side note, this chapter on the mystery school was written solely from Dee's memory in 2014. We didn't know anything about the mystery schools beyond her recollection as a child or if they still existed. Then weeks before the publication of this book, we did a simple internet search to add research on the subject of the mystery schools. We found confirmation of Dee's memory about the schools and the fact that they do indeed still exist. Although there are some differences between the modern mystery school's public information and Dee's recollection of what her dad had told her about the schools, we, of course, left her original story just as she wrote it. We actually had no idea King Solomon was part of the lineage of these schools until we came across their website. The information in the glossary at the end of the book was taken directly from the modern mystery school's website at www.modernmysteryschoolint.com.

Blood Ritual: First Trip Abroad

Dee was less than two years old when she witnessed her first human sacrifice blood ritual.[10] It was during her first international trip with her dad. They were on a plane for hours, and she'd slept during most of the flight in a makeshift bed set up for her. They arrived at a location unknown to her and were greeted by two white men with mustaches and furry hats. One of them spoke to Solomon in English, but they soon turned to each other and spoke in a different language. Dee was able to understand the gist of different languages and whispered what was said to her father. He smiled and quietly told her to be careful not to reveal herself in the presence of others.

They were shuttled directly from the airport to a vast and odd-looking castle. As a young child, Dee was excited to see the castle—for her, it meant they were going to have fun.

"Are we here to have fun?" Dee asked.

"No," her dad replied. "We're here to do what has to be done, so remember to stay focused and don't do any of the things I told you not to do."

"Okay, Dad, I will," she replied.

Solomon and his daughter were ushered into one of the castle's rooms, where several white men in suits were already seated at a huge table. All of the seats were occupied, except the chair at the head of the table. That's where Dee and Solomon sat. Oddly enough, the chair seemed to have been custom-made to allow an adult and child to sit together. The men at the table said some words and gave honor to 'The Mother,' as they looked directly at Dee, and soon the ritual began.

---

[10] The spilling of blood is powerful in the world of magick. Cultures throughout history have made sacrifices to their God deities or idols in order to either please or gain favor with them. There are several different types of blood sacrifice, from the English Blood Brothers Ritual to self-sacrifice, which is the act of spilling your own blood. Death is not uncommon in blood rituals; however, it is usually the death of an animal, or, in the case of the Aztecs and other similar cultures (Toltecs), human sacrifice.

Sacrifice means "to make sacred." The word is derived from two Latin roots: "sacer," meaning "sacred," and "facere," meaning "to make" or "to do." Sacrifice as a "religious" act has five ancient contexts: maintaining the cosmic order, delivering services through gifts, providing protection, commensality, and, finally, mitigating order with chaos (Reverend Thomas). The latter is a more modern idea. While this is speculative at best, it is probably the fifth context, mitigating order with chaos, in which the Freemasons practice blood rituals, in particular, self-sacrifice.

A man in the room stood within a few feet of Solomon and Dee and began speaking while looking directly at Dee. "I voluntarily offer myself for sacrifice," he proclaimed. He was given papers to sign by a man at the table. He spoke again before being handed a knife to perform the final acts of the ritual. The man took the knife and without hesitation, began to stab and cut himself in different places on his body. Blood splattered everywhere, and Dee and her dad were somewhat shielded by two men standing nearby who would block any blood from getting on them.

The ritual was over when the man no longer moved. Then, without any conversation, a man approached and wrote something in Solomon's journal, and he and Dee left for a hotel to await their flight back home. At the hotel, Dee's father asked, "Were you bothered by what you saw today?"

"No," Dee replied.

They had come such a long way, only to witness a horrible self-sacrifice which was never spoken of again. The following morning, they shopped for souvenirs to take home before catching their flight back to the US.

Abuse and Retribution

Solomon and Dee arrived home from their first international trip without incident. Ella's children stormed out of the house as soon as they pulled into the driveway and rushed to the car looking for the gifts Solomon had promised to bring back. They never so much as greeted him or Dee, dismissing them completely, and digging through their bags. Solomon ignored their rudeness and told them to wait until he went inside. He had tried many times in the past to correct their behavior, but it had done no good. No matter what Solomon would say to them, they would ignore him and do whatever they wanted to anyway. But when they started to tease Dee, he made it clear to everyone within hearing range to stop teasing his daughter, and they did. Not only did he have to protect Dee from Ella's mission to thwart her growth, but he also had to protect her from the foolishness of her half-siblings. They were always a very separate part of her life.

Half-Sibling Abuse

On occasion, Ella and Solomon would step out to enjoy an evening out. This time, the four youngest children: Dee, Emma, Deidre, and Fred, were left in the care of Alex, who was around fourteen. Ella instructed Alex to wash the dishes while they were gone. As soon as the car pulled away, Alex picked Dee up and set her on the counter near the sink. The other siblings were left alone to watch television. Dee, at three years old, was the target for abuse as usual.

"I don't want to watch no babies," said Alex.

"You have to; Mom told you," said Dee.

Angrily, Alex grabbed a knife out of the soapy water and cut her on the thigh. Dee looked at him in confusion without crying or complaining. As blood streamed down her leg, Alex grabbed a towel and wrapped it around her thigh. Lifting a still silent Dee off the counter, he took her to her room. "Don't tell, and stay out of sight," he said.

When her parents returned, Solomon went to check on Dee as he normally did, and found her sitting alone with a towel wrapped around the wound on her thigh. He was furious and asked her what had happened. Then Ella walked into the room. "Who did that to Dee?" Ella asked.

"Your son, Alex," Solomon snapped.

Ella went back into the living room and found Alex in front of the television and scolded him. Solomon remained in Dee's room to finish treating the cut, making sure it was properly cleaned up. Ella entered the room just as Solomon left and begged Dee to forgive Alex for what he had done. "He's family. Please don't hurt him," Ella pleaded. Dee didn't respond to her mom, but she never had any intentions of harming her half-sibling Alex.

Dee was a vegan and only ate raw fruits and vegetables. Her dad was aware of her deep connection with nature, and perhaps that's why he raised her as a raw vegan. Her mom would prepare her meals by cleaning and cutting small portions of vegetables and fruits. The other children wanted nothing to do with Dee's raw meals, and would watch in amazement and disgust as Dee would eat a whole lemon along with small portions of raw vegetables. While they ate fried chicken legs and macaroni. Dee loved the taste of fresh vegetables, and couldn't understand why anyone would cook what came from the ground.

That night, Dee hadn't been fed as instructed, so her mom prepared a plate and left it on the table. She overheard her parents arguing again. "We have to do something to suppress Dee," said her mom. "She is dangerous!" Solomon always got angry when Ella talked about suppressing their child. He asked how she had come to be so negative about Dee, and how she had learned about the word 'suppress.' Ella did not answer and merely reiterated that something needed to be done to stop Dee's power. Then the argument got louder, and Dee got up from the table and stayed in her room for the rest of the evening.

Later that night, Solomon went in her room, and he observed that the cut was no longer bleeding. "Very good," he said. Solomon knew that Dee and everyone else in the house had heard the argument between him and Ella, and he tried to explain things to her. "Your mom keeps talking to people who are not on your side, but I love you above all else," he said. He tucked her in and used his finger to draw lines in her hand before she went to sleep.

Years later as an adult, Alex apologized for how he had treated his youngest half-sibling Dee, and he was the only person to do so. The scar from the knife cut remains on her leg to this day as a reminder.

Half-Sibling Abuse and Retribution

Dee's mom often spent her time in her own room with the door closed, particularly if Solomon was not home. This time when her dad had left, Deidre decided to play "doctor" with Dee, who was four years old. Although Dee had no idea what the game entailed, she was happy to finally be included in playing with the other children.

Deidre took needles from her mother's sewing kit and called her other siblings into her room. She began sticking needles into Dee's arm, and nobody said a word to stop her. They merely looked on in horrified delight, not at the abuse, but at Dee's lack of tears or complaints. Dee just silently observed them as Deidre abused her. Deidre turned to her brothers and sisters and said, "See, she's not like us! She isn't even crying. Dee doesn't feel pain like us," she proclaimed.

Solomon arrived home to find Dee bleeding yet again, and after quickly treating her, another heated argument ensued between him and his wife. He was furious because Ella had no control over her own children, and she didn't want him to discipline them at all. Whenever one of the half-siblings abused Dee, Ella would always speak to Dee privately and ask her to forgive them, under the pretext that they were family. This time she did not.

Soon after, Dee was at home with her mom and half-siblings again. Dee was drawing in her coloring book on the couch and Deidre was at her mother's sewing machine. "When I'm done sewing this blouse, we're going to play doctor again," Deidre told her cheerfully. Dee knew what "playing doctor" meant from her last experience and she didn't like it. So Dee focused her attention on Deidre's fingers without actually thinking of harming her. Suddenly she saw that Deidre's fingers had slid under the sewing machine needle as it was moving up and down. Deidre howled in pain for her mother and gasped at Dee as she clutched her sewn together fingers. "She made me stick my fingers under the needle!" Deidre screamed to her mother. Ella glanced over at Dee but didn't say a word.

She took Deidre to the bathroom to tend to the injury, while Deidre cried out in pain. Once finished, she sent Deidre to her room and angrily scolded Dee for what she had done.

"Deidre was going to play doctor and try to hurt me again," explained Dee.

Waving her excuse away, Ella said, "You can hurt Deidre and others far more than they can hurt you. Never do that again!"

After that day, Deidre never tried to physically hurt Dee, but she continued to trick her and steal from her every chance she could.

Physical Abuse by Ella

It seemed that every time Dee was home alone without her dad, she was subjected to trauma or teasing. At only five years old, Dee was taking her usual nap and exploring the universe with the boy of her dreams when Ella entered her room. Although Dee was out of her body, her eyes were open, and she was aware of her mom's presence in her room. At times Dee would quickly leave her body and forget to close her eyes. Solomon observed this and advised her to take the time to close her eyes first. He even gently closed them for her when she forgot. Dee was in the process of saying goodbye to the boy of her dreams and returning to her body when suddenly, Ella shook her by the shoulders and began slapping her in the face, all while screaming, "Come back! Come back!"

Solomon returned home in time to catch Ella in the act of abusing their child. He rushed into Dee's room when he heard the yells and smacks, terrified of what he'd find. He was devastated to see Ella standing over Dee abusing her while she was out of the body. He rushed to stop his wife before she did more damage, and with a firm grip pulled her away from their young daughter. He shouted at her to leave, as he stood guarding Dee with his fists clenched. Ella silently left the room, and her dad waited for Dee to return to her body and made sure she was unhurt. Afterwards, a loud argument ensued yet again between him and Ella.

"What the hell were you doing to Dee?" Solomon demanded to know.

"She sleeps too much for a child," Ella protested.

"That's what some children do, Ella! I told you she's not like other children. You could cause permanent damage to her brain," he said.

"We need to suppress her!" Ella shrieked.

Solomon lowered his voice. "I don't know what you have been told, but if I ever see or hear you doing this again, there will be consequences."

Dee didn't want to hear her parents argue any longer, so she went to the back yard and sat alone for a long time.

The next day she asked her mom and dad separately why the family was so hateful towards her. Her dad told her, "They are not your real brothers and sisters, and you should try to keep that in mind." On the other hand, her mom reiterated what she had stated numerous times before, "You need to forgive all bad things done and never hurt anyone."

Dee's Foot Injury

Solomon hired construction workers to do some work on the exterior of their house. Dee, being naturally curious decided to wander outside to watch the men. She skipped along to the side of the house and mistakenly stepped on a nail protruding from a piece of wood. The nail went all the way through her small foot, but she felt no pain. She hobbled to the porch with the piece of wood and nail still attached to her foot to sit and remove it. A construction worker spotted her and grabbed her hand before she could pull it out. "Wait for your mom, little girl!" he said. Dee was four or five years old at the time and tried to pull her hand away from the man. He looked at her oddly and screamed for her mom because Solomon was out of town.

Ella and Deidre came out and took Dee into the house. "Don't remove that nail, Dee, you might cause more damage," her mom warned. "I'm going to take you to the emergency room." Deidre had a curious look on her face as she watched Dee and said, "She's just weird. Look at her. She isn't even complaining or crying about the big nail in her foot." Ella disregarded Deidre as she picked Dee up and put her in the car. Deidre was following close behind. "I want to see what she does when the doctor removes it!" yelled Deidre. "No," said Ella. "You stay at home with Alex and help watch Emma and Fred." Deidre got angry and ran into the house, slamming the door behind her.

When Dee and her mom were seen by the doctor, he wanted to give Dee a shot, but her mom told him not to. "She has never had any shots or taken any medicine. Her dad thinks it will harm her, so please don't give her anything." The doctor briefly stared at Ella, and then at Dee, as she sat calmly with the nail protruding from her foot. "Hold her down and block her from watching as I pull the nail out," said the doctor. Ella did as instructed, but Dee kept trying to push her mom out the way so she could see. The nail was pulled out, and the doctor looked at her calmness in amazement. "You have a courageous daughter," he said. The doctor treated the wound and offered them medication, but her mom declined again.

When they returned home, Dee removed the cream the doctor had put on her wound and used some paste the Shaman had given her for cuts and bruises. The doctor told Dee not to walk on her foot for a week. But the next day she was walking as if nothing had happened. Her foot was healed.

Trips with Ella

Ella was involved with the Order of the Eastern Star[11]. Solomon believed the contact was made through her prior relationships with men who were loosely affiliated with Masonic organizations. Solomon himself was not an active member of this organization, at least as far as Dee knew. But what could she really know about her dad's affiliations when she was just a child? Despite Ella's efforts to maintain a veil of secrecy, Solomon was aware of her association and communications with the order outside of her regular planned activities. He tried to speak with her about the group, but it was completely useless. Ella became so belligerent at times; it was as though her entire personality would change. Her anger was such that he did not want to be anywhere near when she was in that state. He knew there was nothing he could do to change her mind about the organization or her views, as it had been too long since "they" had a hold of her, so he eventually stopped trying.

Ella took Dee to the Eastern Star gatherings several times without Solomon's knowledge. Dee observed the uniforms they wore and the things

---

[11] The order of the Eastern Star has a tangled history. Originally conceived as an American form of adoptive Masonry as early as the 1840's, it took until 1876 for the General Grand chapter, Order of the Eastern Star, to be formed. There are at least two separate organizations that both say that they are dedicated to the unification of all Eastern Stars, but which lead a separate existence from the General Grand chapter and were founded in 1947 and 1962 respectively. There is also an African-American organization, dating from the days when American Masons officially barred blacks from membership.

The Eastern Stars of Freemasonry also goes back to Egypt and the worship of the female deity Aset (Isis). The female is the Eastern Star because Isis, the wife of Osiris, had to travel eastward to find Osiris's body after his brother, Set, had killed him. Osiris had to be resurrected for revenge through his son, Horus, who was also called "The Horizon."

they did at the gatherings. She thought they were just a bunch of women playing games and dressing up in costumes until her father told her they were doing rituals so that they might increase in rank. Dee had no idea what he meant, and would always stand near the doorway and refuse to go any further inside. She just didn't like the energy and kept her distance from everyone.

Dee once observed the women at the gathering lined up to enter a large room, Ella among them. Together they created a sort of cup and saucer formation. There was an empty chair in the middle, and Ella left the formation to try to get Dee to sit in the chair. Dee was five at the time and swung her arms wildly while screaming for her mom to leave her alone. No one else dared to approach her, and Ella eventually gave up. So the women did the ritual with an empty chair, as Dee observed from her position near the door. Only a few members of the group were black (most were white), and all of the higher-ranking members sitting in chairs against the wall and observing were white. Although Dee never saw any other children at the gatherings, she heard some of the higher-ranking members tell Ella to always bring her child along. Ella never took any of her other children with her to gatherings.

In addition to taking Dee to Eastern Star gatherings, Ella would also try to take her to see different doctors when Solomon left her at home. She recalls going to several places with her mom and refusing to get out of the car. Ella once took her to a medical complex, and when she refused to get out, Ella went inside and came back with two white men in lab coats. Dee rolled down her window and told the men to stay away, and they complied with her demands. Her mom also took her to school to try and register her, even though Solomon told her that public school was not the place for her to learn anything. Dee stayed in the car and refused to get out. Once at home, she always told her dad about the occurrences with her mom, and another argument would ensue between her parents. Ultimately, Dee stopped telling her dad about the things that were done to her because she didn't want her parents to argue anymore.

Solomon's Generosity and Dee's Retribution

Solomon was by nature a very generous man, and he would often do things for Ella's children just to make them feel happy. He hoped that by showing special affection towards them, they would accept his child and stop tormenting her. Through his connections, he made it possible for one of Ella's sons to have a chance to join the Special Forces, even though there were very few black soldiers in the program at the time. Solomon tried to encourage Ella's son to do something else, but the youngster was insistent about joining, so Solomon did everything he could to make sure it happened. He arranged for Alex, who always got good grades in school, to attend the college of his choice. Her dad also purchased two new cars: a new Mustang for one of Ella's oldest sons and a new Grand Am for James. When he handed over the keys to James, who was in his late teens, he ran out of the house in excitement to see his new car and knocked Dee down in the process.

Dee lay there looking at him and said, "Hey, you knocked me down and hurt me!" He ignored her complaint and stepped over her and out of the door without saying anything. Her dad had just bought him a new car, but that didn't stop him from being cruel to her. The next time Dee saw James, she reminded him and said, "You hurt me when you knocked me down, and you didn't apologize."

"I'm not apologizing to you," he said with a smirk.

"I will give you one week," Dee warned.

"Whatever," he said, dismissing her as if she meant nothing.

The week passed, and no apology was forthcoming. One day while James was on his way out again, he noticed Dee staring at him. "What the hell are you looking at?" he asked. Dee gave no reply, so he rolled his eyes and shut the door behind him.

Dee immediately ran to her room and sat with her crayons and a blank piece of paper. Then she slowly drew a picture of James' car stuck in a tree. A few hours later the phone rang, and when nobody answered it the first time, someone called right back. Ella finally answered. It was James, and he was in distress. He told her that he had wrecked his car but had only sustained minor injuries. Ella gathered Emma, Fred, and Dee to pick him up at the site of the accident not far from the house. When Ella pulled up, they saw James' car suspended in the limbs of a tree and no one could figure out how it got there. Ella took them all back home, and Dee ran to her room to throw away the picture she had drawn of James' car in a tree before anyone found out about her magick. Neither James nor Ella ever suspected her of having anything to do with the incident.

Solomon was Dee's only confidant, guide, and protector. In contrast, Solomon knew that Ella would do everything she could, either on a conscious or manipulated level, to hinder and undermine their child's development. It was clear that Ella had been taught to fear Dee's powers and to suppress her anyway her "handlers" instructed. Handlers were those who controlled Ella and filled her head with false information. At times he considered taking Dee out of the US, but he knew "they" would have made Ella suffer even more, and he loved her too much for that. Ella was so influenced by her handlers that she did not want Solomon's protection. When he offered to take them all away, Ella was unyielding in her rejection. With that in mind, he continued his mission to make sure his child was protected so that she would reach her full human potential.

The Mason Gathering

Solomon's status with the Freemasons was unknown, but he would sometimes attend gatherings at their request. Many members thanked him for the services he had provided them over the years. Through his advice, he had helped many of them become successful in many ventures, as he was exceptional with numbers. A favorite phrase of his which he often used was, "Everything is numbers."

Dee was around four years old when her dad took her to a gathering at the request of a Freemason leader. He kept her in his arms the whole time, as she was the only child among all the men. They all bowed to Solomon and Dee in honor of their presence.

One of the men, who was purported to have psychic powers, approached Solomon. "If the forces had not interfered with the mother of the child, you would have had many children with great powers," he said. Solomon responded right away. "I am in the line of the Egyptian sun god, Ra. The Ancients have told me that I was to have only one divine girl child with my wife."

The man backed away without saying another word, but other members had seen the confrontation and the head of the group got wind of it soon after. The man who had challenged Solomon was subsequently disciplined. The leader of the group, as well as others, profusely apologized to Solomon, mortified at the disrespect shown to him and his daughter. They further thanked him for honoring them with their presence at the gathering. The leader wrote something in journal, and they left.

Solomon knew Dee had heard what the man had said about her mom. So on the way home that night, he explained how he had received a vision of Ella, and knew about her mom long before they actually met. He told her the stories of how he would watch Ella and of their eventual meeting at the train station.

The Probing

Solomon approached Ella and told her they would have to take Dee to see both a doctor and a psychiatrist. He was not at all fond of the idea, but "they" had requested he bring her. To keep them appeased, and more importantly, to accomplish his mission to gain entry for Dee into the mystery schools, he agreed to a very limited examination.

He took Dee to the doctor first and whispered, "Don't answer any questions, and if they poke you just pretend that it hurts." Dee went into the exam room alone, and a nurse and doctor were inside waiting. The nurse was a younger woman in her 30's, and every time she spoke, her nose would twitch. The doctor was an older man wearing a white lab coat. They performed a series of examinations, and just as her dad had warned, they poked her, and she reacted with an "ouch," even though it did not hurt. Solomon was called into the room because they wanted to do some additional tests. He refused. "That was not part of the agreement. We are leaving." He picked her up and left. Nothing else was said.

The next stop was at the psychiatrist's office, and again her dad explained what she had to do. "You have to go inside the doctor's office alone, but keep the door open so that I can monitor what's going on." As instructed, she entered the psychiatrist's office and left the door open. She sat down in the chair in front of the desk; looking back to be sure she could still see her father in the waiting room.

The doctor did not say anything for a long time; he just kept shuffling papers on his desk as Dee waited patiently. Then he initiated an inkblot test, producing three cards.

"What do you see on the cards?" he asked.

"I see a paper that looks like something black had been spilled on it," said Dee.

"You don't understand. I want you to tell me if you see an image on the cards," the doctor said.

"What am I supposed to see?" Dee asked.

"Just look at it carefully and tell me," said the doctor.

"I am looking at it carefully, and I see black stuff spilled on white paper," she said.

The doctor attempted a different tack and said, "Other children have seen things like a birdhouse with grass, or a broken glass and spilled milk. Do you see anything like that?" Dee was curious about the number of children he saw, and asked, "How many other children did you show these cards to?" "Many," he said. "That's my job." Dee looked back to see Solomon in the waiting room. "Focus your attention on me," the doctor instructed, as he put the cards down. "Do you know what imagination is?"

"Imagination is when you think about things that are not really there," she said.

"Well, that's sort of right. Tell me about your dreams," said the doctor.

With a jolt, Dee sat upright in the chair and said, "My dreams are mine alone and if you were supposed to know about them, you already would."

The psychiatrist huffed, "You need to tell me about your dreams so that I can help you understand them."

She turned to look at her dad again, and he shook his head to indicate "No." So Dee said, "I'm tired, and I want to go home." The doctor jotted down notes in his book and extended his hand to her so that they would walk out the door together. She ducked under his hand and ran to her dad, clinging to his leg until he picked her up. The psychiatrist requested to speak with her dad alone. Solomon placed the reluctant Dee into her mom's arms and followed the doctor into his office, closing the door behind them.

They were not in the office long before Dee heard her dad exclaim, "Hell, no!" in an unusually piercing tone for him. Her mom jumped, almost dropping poor Dee on the floor. Solomon flew out of the office with the doctor at his heels. He wanted to make another appointment for Dee, but Solomon sternly refused and said, "This was a one-time visit. We will not be returning!"

"I still have to call and let them know," said the doctor.

"You can do whatever you please, but we are leaving," said Solomon.

That was the last time Solomon ever took Dee to see any doctors.

Racist Cop

Unfortunately, most black Americans living in the south and other places in America have had experiences with racist cops at one time or another. Dee witnessed this at the young age of three or four years old. Simply put, racism was largely based on the hatred that some white Americans had toward blacks. This was the world Dee was born into, and it still exists to this very day. Solomon lived and experienced a sort of second-class citizenship throughout his life in the US, regardless of his money or stature.

One day Solomon was taking Dee and Ella to visit an aunt in Mississippi. The other children had refused to go because Aunt Anna did not have indoor plumbing, and the thought of using an outhouse was just too much for them. While driving along the highway, a police car pulled up behind them. Solomon had not broken any traffic laws but was not surprised when the red flashing lights of the patrol car came on. "It's probably a small-town racist cop," he said. Solomon pulled over, and the cop approached with his gun drawn.

He ordered Dee's father to get out, and Solomon complied by stepping slowly from the vehicle. Dee heard the cop tell her dad that he would not allow him to travel down "his" road any longer. Solomon tried to explain that he was simply heading to a relative's home who lived in the state. The cop replied by cursing at him and announcing he was taking his "nigger ass" to jail for speaking out of turn.

Concerned for her father's well-being and wanting the cop to go away, Dee decided to use her magick. She didn't want to hurt the cop, so she closed her eyes and focused on the man's belly, causing him to pass gas. The cop didn't seem bothered and stood his ground while passing gas with his gun still pointed at her dad. Seeing this in her mind's eye, Dee took it a step further by making the cop's bowels loosen, and he was forced to squeeze his legs tightly together. He was resilient, still holding his ground as he soiled himself. She focused more on the cop making him soil himself until his bowels were completely empty. He grabbed the back of his pants, looked around in confusion, and at last acquiesced, sending Solomon on his way while he waddled awkwardly to his patrol car with lots of poop in his pants.

Solomon got back in the car and noticed that Dee's eyes were closed and her mom was watching her intensely. Ella seemed to always know when Dee was using her gifts. Dee finally opened her eyes, and her mom immediately began scolding her. "Never do things like that again!" Ella screamed. Her dad smiled and reached over the seat to bring her up front with him.

"What did you do to the cop?" Solomon asked.

"I made him poop on himself so he would leave you alone," replied Dee. Solomon could not help but laugh.

Her mom, however, was worried, and whispered to him over the seat, "We need to suppress her power."

Ella only possessed an elementary school education, and she often spoke about suppressing Dee, genuinely believing that it was the best thing to do. "You're always saying we need to suppress Dee. Where did you learn that word from anyway?" Solomon asked. Ella would never answer him.

They continued on their way and soon arrived at Aunt Anna and Uncle Mickey's house. Solomon would always bring lots of expensive liquor and beer along during his visits, and many people showed up when he was in town. He would also give Aunt Anna money for cooking, as she was an extraordinary cook and made delicious meals. Ella always complained. "My sister is just poor country folk. You're giving them too much," she would say. "That's nonsense," was Solomon's only reply.

During the get-together, Dee's dad would slowly sip his drink while watching everyone enjoying themselves. Dee sat on the couch and was smiling from ear to ear, always having a happy demeanor and glad to be with her dad. Uncle Mickey was sitting at a table and noticed her smiling. He grabbed his cane and began to approach her. Dee knew he was coming to pinch her cheek, which she didn't like. So when he got halfway to her, Dee used her magick and made his cane disappear, only to reappear back at the table where he had been sitting. Uncle Mickey stopped in his tracks, and Solomon saw him.

"What are you doing walking around without your cane, Mickey?"

Mickey shrugged his shoulders. "I don't know."

"He had it with him when he got up. I don't know how it wound up back at the table. This is some good liquor you brought us," said Mickey's friend, who was sitting next to him.

Solomon smiled. "Where were you going, Mickey?"

"I saw Dee sitting on the couch smiling. I was just going over to pinch her cheek," he said.

Solomon turned to Dee with a grin as if he knew what she had done. "How many times do I have to tell you; she doesn't like to be touched," he said jokingly. Her dad sat next to her for the duration of the party, and they had a laugh together.

The Cabin and the Beach House

Dee discovered how to levitate her body when she was a baby. She would float her physical body above her bed because she found it more comfortable than sleeping on the mattress.

Solomon came home late one evening and saw her floating in the air above her bed. Although her body was asleep, Dee could feel and see her dad's presence. She had her own room, and a canopy surrounded her bed for privacy. Her dad didn't want to wake her, so he lifted the canopy above her and tied it together so she would not hit the ceiling. Dee smiled, thinking his actions were silly.

The next morning, Solomon told her, "I saw you floating above your bed last night. When did you learn how to do that?"

"Not long ago," she replied calmly.

"That's really great, but you should not do that anymore in this house because someone may see you," he explained. "You can do those things at the cabin."

Solomon's hunting cabin was in a remote area. There wasn't much for children to do, but he once took Ella's two youngest children, Emma and Fred, along. They complained so much that he had to take them back home the same day. Dee, on the other hand, loved the cabin and enjoyed hanging out with her dad. He would let her burn wood in the fireplace until it got so hot inside, that he and his friend, Ross, would go outside just to cool off.

Each time they went to the cabin, her dad would first walk towards the two special trees. He would then pick up a stick that he would leave lying between the trees, and he would draw a circle around one tree, scratching the letter "M" in the circle with the tip of the stick. He would then close his eyes and lift his head to the sky for a few moments before repeating the process with the second tree, only instead of the letter "M," it was the letter "F."

Solomon noticed Dee watching him one day and called her over. "Why do you draw circles around the trees?" Dee asked. "I'm honoring the ancestors; it's very important," he replied. "When I was a little boy, my father took me to this cabin, and we planted these two trees together. My father told me I needed to take care of them, and one day they would grow to be big and strong, and I could share their beginnings with my own family. The letter 'M' is for 'mother' and 'F' is for 'father.' This is my way of honoring my parents." Dee thought this was a beautiful way to show honor, and promised her father that she would carry on his tradition. So whenever they went to the cabin from then on, Dee would complete the same ritual with the trees as her dad.

Solomon also had a beach house on Dauphin Island in Alabama that he would take Ella and all the children to visit at times. The house was on stilts and situated right near the ocean. During their first visit, when Dee was a small child, she remembers sitting near the front door and sucking her thumb, as she watched her half-siblings run around the house exploring. They were jumping on the couch, claiming which room they wanted to sleep in and eventually ended up in her dad's library. The library was two levels, and there was a big ladder on wheels that could move around the room to reach the books.

They began to push each other on the ladder until Solomon entered and put a stop to it. "No one is allowed in my library. Go help your mother unload the bags from the car," he said. Dee stayed by the door until her dad picked her up and sat her on the couch. After they all settled in, her mom walked out to the wrap-around deck and sat watching the ocean, and Dee and her dad joined her. Ella seemed to like the house as much as her children, and her husband asked if she wanted to move into the home.

"I would like to visit, but I would never move away from my friends in town," Ella replied. Then Wilson came out to the deck and asked if they could go outside to the water.

"Wait until tomorrow; we need to go shopping for food," Solomon said. His other siblings started to complain, and her dad advised them all that the people in that area were very snobbish. "We're the only black folks in this area, so don't act foolish when you do go outside."

After a while, they went to the stores, heading for the fish market first. Solomon's favorite was octopus, and while he searched for the delicacy, Ella selected some fish that she liked. They also purchased a lot of crab legs and crawfish. The last stop was another market where they bought many other grocery items. They arrived back at the beach house and unloaded the groceries. Ella gave her husband a big kiss and lifted Dee up and hugged her. She seemed pleased as she began preparing the meal, and once everything was done, everybody sat down to eat.

All the children sat at a table while Ella and Solomon went to the deck to dine. Dee was eating mashed up vegetables and drinking breast milk. Deidre looked at Dee and shook her head in disgust, but Wilson, Fred, Emma, Betty and Alex were too busy eating crab legs to join in with picking on Dee. Betty, who was Ella's oldest daughter, began swelling up while eating the crab legs. Wilson called out for his mother, and she and Solomon came inside. Ella saw Betty's swollen face and didn't know what was wrong until Solomon said, "You're allergic to shellfish; don't eat any more of that." He gave her an elixir he made from some of the herbs that he always carried with him. Then he made a bath and told her to get into it. They left the next day, which was much earlier than expected because Ella wanted to take Betty to a doctor. They would all visit the beach house together a few times a year, and everyone looked forward to going.

Soon after that trip to the beach, her dad received a visit from his oldest son Solomon Jr. Her dad had three sons with his former wife, and they were all estranged from him. Her dad was disappointed in Solomon Jr., and would often tell him that he was no son of his. But that did little to stop his son's occasional trips from California to Alabama to visit him. Dee heard her father say many times that if Solomon Jr. paid him a visit; he was either in trouble or needed money. He had gotten Solomon Jr. and people associated with him out of many bad situations in the past, and he was tired of getting involved.

During the visits, her dad would not allow Solomon Jr. inside the house, and they spoke in the front yard. On this visit, Ella insisted that Solomon invite his son inside to talk, and with much hesitation, he allowed it. Solomon Jr. greeted all of Ella's children except Dee because she kept her distance and avoided him. Her dad had told her many times to never think of his sons as family because they could never be that. Solomon Jr. seemed to have taken an interest in Ella's oldest daughter, Betty. So when her dad was on the phone or preoccupied with something else, Solomon Jr. and Betty would speak with each other.

Betty was 11 years old, and she found out that Solomon Jr. had children around her age. Dee doesn't know how it came to be, but the next thing she heard was Betty begging her mom to let her live with Solomon Jr.

in California. Solomon Jr. said that he would allow her to live with him, and surprisingly Ella agreed without any reluctance or skepticism. Her dad was livid with Solomon Jr. for his offer to keep Betty, and they stepped outside to have a private conversation outside.

When Solomon returned, he seemed a bit emotional and asked his wife. "Why would you allow your 11-year-old daughter to live with complete strangers who are not even blood-related?"

"They are my children," Ella advised matter-of-factly. "I alone will be making all the decisions for them."

"You will be putting your daughter in harm's way if you allow her to leave," said Solomon.

Betty approached her mother in the midst of their discussion and pleaded. "Please, Mom, I want to live in California with Solomon Jr., and you said you would let me."

"I haven't changed my mind," Ella told Betty. "Go get all your things packed up so you can go with him."

Solomon did not give up, and an argument ensued between them, as Solomon Jr. waited outside. Betty packed all of her belongings and was ready to leave, and Solomon continued to criticize Ella's decision. He tirelessly tried to get Ella to see the error of her ways, but it was no use. "I don't trust Solomon Jr. so why should you trust him with your 11-year-old daughter?" He asked. Ella was silent, and he continued. "Those people in California don't like you or your children, so why are you allowing this?" Ella waved her hand in disregard of Solomon and said, "They are my children. That's why!" Solomon gave up and sat without saying another word as Ella helped put Betty's luggage in Solomon Jr.'s vehicle.

That was the last time Dee saw Betty for several years, and when Solomon Jr. visited Alabama every so often, he would never bring Betty along with him. Apparently, Betty wasn't interested in seeing her mother, and it seemed that Ella wasn't interested in seeing Betty either. Solomon had tried numerous times to get Ella to call Betty or visit her in California. He even went so far as to make all the arrangement in advance for her to visit, but Ella didn't want to go. So he left it alone.

The Cabin: Struck by Lightning

Almost every time Solomon went to the hunting cabin, Dee went along with him. The deer hunting trip with his friend Ross was no exception. Ross had been having difficulties with his family, and Solomon offered him the cabin as a temporary living space. He had been there for a few weeks when Dee and Solomon arrived for the hunting trip. They set out on the hunt, and after a while, they came upon a deer.

"Stay here, Little D," her dad whispered. Solomon watched Ross inch closer to a tree as he took aim with his crossbow, and the deer was felled.

A light rain began to fall, and Ross thought it was better to take the deer to the smaller cabin on the property, as it was much closer. Solomon did not agree. "We should head back to the main cabin," he said. After hearing them, Dee said, "A big storm is coming soon, and there will be lots of rain and lights in the sky." As if on cue, the sky opened up, and heavy rain began to fall, with big bolts of lightning and loud claps of thunder. "Hey, how did she know about the thunderstorm?" Ross asked. Solomon completely ignored the question and said, "You're right, we should go to the smaller cabin after all."

The two men took the deer to a covered area near the smaller cabin to prepare it. Ross had planned to take all the deer meat to his family. Dee loved the storm and asked if she could play outside while they worked. Solomon agreed but told her to stay close. Dee relished in the storm, feeling the rain on her face and the sound of the leaves blowing in the wind.

Suddenly, lightning struck her, and she fell to the ground, paralyzed. As she lay there unable to move, the wind began to blow around her, and in an instant, she was out of her body and merged with the wind to become one. The scene around her became very bright, so bright it blinded her, and all she could see was darkness. Unafraid, Dee focused on the darkness, wanting to see what was beyond. Soon the darkness cleared and it became bright once again. Her energy continued to flow with the wind and lightning, and in this state, she was somehow able to see the whole planet and every person and animal in it all at once. It was reminiscent of the first vision she had at one year old. At that time, she was able to be in the presence of every animal in the world all at once, and it made her feel good. She understood that wild animals were more true to their purpose than human beings, and that realization made her want to visit wild animals from that point on.

Ross saw her get struck and immediately ran to her side, yelling for Solomon. Her dad kneeled to check her for injuries. Dee was aware and could see and hear everything happening around her, but was still out of her body. Ross said, "We need to get her to a hospital. I saw her get struck by a lightning bolt." Dee knew Solomon was waiting for her to return, and that helped her come back sooner. She began to stir a bit.

"Are you all right?" Solomon asked.

"Yes, I'm fine," she said. Dee tried to sit up but was still unable to do so.

"Stay on the ground until you're ready to move," her dad whispered.

Ross was worried and continued to urge Solomon to take her to the hospital. He couldn't understand why Solomon did not seem worried about his daughter. "Don't worry; I know what I'm doing," said Solomon. As she continued to recover on the ground, Ross exclaimed, "It's a miracle! A tiny little girl gets struck by a giant lightning bolt and not only survives but doesn't sustain a single injury. I have to tell someone. I have to tell everyone!"

Dee didn't like what Ross was saying, and she knew that her dad would like it even less. She quickly sat upright and said, "Dad, can I have some water?" He hurried to retrieve some water, and as she drank, Ross pulled Solomon aside. "I'm worried because that was a massive lightning bolt that struck her. You know how many volts are in that thing? We should tell someone right away," he repeated. Solomon stared at Ross intensely. "If you speak to anyone about this incident, you will be harmed because 'they' already know about her." Ross seemed confused by his explanation, but Solomon declined to explain any further. When Dee had fully recovered, they finished preparing the deer and returned to the main cabin.

Days later, Dee heard Solomon telling his best friend U what had happened at the cabin, and subsequently to Ross. His friend Ross had gone to a newspaper reporter to tell the story anyway, completely ignoring Solomon's warning. The following day, both Ross and the reporter were found dead. Dee doesn't have any information as to why or how they died but remembers thinking it was a strange coincidence.

47

Later that evening, as Dee and her dad sat together, he asked her about her experience when she had been struck by lightning.

"I was floating around, and I could see all the people and animals in the whole world all at once, very softly," she said.

"What do you mean when you say 'softly'?" Solomon asked.

"Like feeling a cushion," she said.

Her dad smiled, and Dee told him about seeing all the wild animals and how good it made her feel to be with them. Solomon promised to take her to visit wild animals in the future. He would also take her to the Shaman soon so that she could talk more with him about her experience.

The Cabin: Spider Bites

Dee and Solomon were off on another trip to the cabin, but not to hunt. Her dad picked up his best friend U to take along with them. U was a large black man that had a serious demeanor. Dee called him Uncle U, and Solomon had left Dee in his care several times when she was just a baby, and he had business to take care of. At times he thought it was better to leave her with U rather than Ella. It had been a while since Dee had seen U because he had moved to Texas. U always made Dee laugh, and she looked forward to seeing him again.

While at the cabin, Solomon and U were sitting near the fireplace enjoying cigars. Dee went to ask her dad if she could play outside but paused when she noticed a third cigar burning on the hearth. "Who's that for?" Dee asked, and Solomon laughed. "It's for the boy of your dreams," he exclaimed. Dee's father knew she had daily dreams and visions of a little boy, and they all laughed, and everyone was happy.

Dee was especially delighted because she could do whatever she wanted to in the relative privacy of the cabin's property. She ran out to the woods to chase butterflies until she grew tired. Then she decided to levitate in the air and look at the bugs and little insects on the trees. It was one of her favorite things to do while at the cabin.

It wasn't long before she heard her dad calling her. As she was descending to the ground, she heard an animal in the bushes behind her. She quickly landed, wanting to see what it was – causing a small catastrophe. She had planned to land on a log she had spotted, but was distracted by the sound in the bushes. Turning toward the noise, she lost her footing on the log and fell into a hole in the ground. It wasn't very deep, but she was only four years old and not very tall. She completely forgot about levitating out of the hole and began grabbing at the vines around her to try and pull herself out. Dimly she realized that the hole was full of spider webs and their tenants! They crawled all over her as she continued her struggle to get out.

U and Solomon had already begun to look for her. U spotted her first, snatching her out of the hole while calling out to Solomon. Dee was covered with spiders, and her dad quickly stripped her down to her underwear. Now some of them were crawling on her bare skin. "Those spiders are poisonous; we need to get them off right away," U said with urgency. They wiped them away, stomping on them when they fell to the ground. One spider managed to find its way into her nostril. Her dad reached into his medicine bag, which he carried around his neck. He took out what appeared to be a dart. He poked the spider, and it was removed, but not before it bit her nose. Dee watched calmly and quietly as they helped her.

The poison was quick to act, and her face was affected first, quickly swelling. Her legs became numb, and she crumpled to the forest ground in a heap, her body shaking uncontrollably. U panicked. "Dee has been paralyzed, Solomon! The spiders' toxins are spreading. We have to get her to a hospital now!" he advised, his voice giving away how terrified he truly was. Dee stopped shaking and suddenly became stiff like a board. Solomon remained calm and knelt down while holding her hand. He whispered, "You're going to be fine, and you have the ability to heal yourself." It was something in the way her dad said those words that made Dee know what to do, and before long, she was feeling better. "I can feel my legs again," she said.

Solomon gently picked her up and carried her inside the cabin to her room. She had been bitten multiple times and had welts all over her little body. He cleaned the bites and rubbed an ointment from his medicine bag onto her skin. U was still worried about the venom and stepped inside to see how she was doing. He felt that she should be taken to the hospital. Solomon asked him to wait outside because he would speak with him after he'd treated the bites.

U waited anxiously outside her door. When Solomon appeared, U began to plead his case again. "I really think that we should take her to the hospital, Solomon. I know from experience that a lot of those spiders were poisonous." Solomon shook his head. "It's not necessary for her to go to the hospital. She is capable of healing herself. You'll see shortly."

While Solomon was explaining things to U, Dee was busy with the process of healing. She squeezed her hands into tight little fists and was able to force the toxins out of her body and skin. She watched the welts on her skin go down as liquid came out of her pores. In no time she was back to her healthy self. She went to wash her skin and then played quietly on the bed with her toys. U went to check on her after having spoken with Solomon and found her at play, perfectly fine. All evidence of the spider bites were gone.

Solomon came to the doorway, but U stopped him before he could approach Dee. U gave him an effusive handshake and congratulations, seemingly astonished at her miraculous healing, and at what Solomon had revealed to him about Dee. She watched the exchange between the two men and her dad said, "I've told U some of our secrets, and he will be traveling with us from now on."

Solomon checked on Dee again and saw that she was perfectly fine. The men adjourned to the fireplace, but U kept returning to Dee's room marveling over her healing.

Group Healing

One of Solomon's favorite things to do was listening to the blues. He attended jam sessions at a recording studio often enough that he was as familiar with the staff as they were with him. He took Dee along to one of these sessions once and sat her down in the control room. "Don't touch any of the buttons on the console. You can watch the men play through the window," her dad said. Happy with this arrangement, she sat on the couch and delighted in the music, as Solomon joined the other men in the studio. Ella never attended any of the jam sessions with Solomon but has been particularly fond of one of the musicians who played there. So when the time came for their next trip, Ella decided to join them and had a chance to meet all the musicians and get their autographs.

When they returned home, Solomon opened the car trunk to unload some things they had purchased while they were out, and left it open as he carried the bags inside. Dee was playing around the car with a ball and had placed her foot on the bumper to fix her shoe laces. Solomon returned to close the trunk and didn't notice Dee nearby. He inadvertently slammed the trunk hard on her toe and walked away. Dee calmly called out to him but he was too busy in his own thoughts and didn't hear her.

Luckily, Ella came outside and saw Dee's foot caught in the trunk. Frantically, she screamed for Solomon who came running in an instant. When her dad saw Dee' foot stuck in the trunk, he fumbled with his keys, trying to open it as quickly as possible. Dee watched in calm silence wondering why her dad was rushing. *I'm not hurt or anything; I'm just stuck,* she thought.

At last, her foot was free, and she immediately felt pressure but no intense pain despite the fact that her toe was severely damaged and bleeding. Deidre had come out of the house to investigate her mother's screams. When she saw Dee's injury, she smiled wickedly and said, "See, she's not even crying. She's different!" Deidre ran down the street telling anyone who would listen about Dee being different. Ella and Solomon ignored her, as they carried Dee into the house. He rubbed a salve the Shaman had given to him on her toe, as Dee watched without complaint.

Solomon frowned. "It's pretty bad, Ella. We need to help her heal right away." Ella was reluctant and looked around to be sure no one was nearby to witness what he was asking her to take part in before agreeing. The three of them held hands as Solomon began chanting incantations. Then right before their eyes, they witnessed the bleeding stop and her wound close up. Her big toe was still red, and the nail was still split from her skin. Dee still has the split toenail to this day that serves as a reminder.

Solomon's Special Chair

Dee was now about five years old and had been going to the cabin on a regular basis for quite a while. Solomon informed Ella that they would be leaving again on another trip and would meet up with U at the cabin. They would remain for about a week because there was work to be done.

By the time Solomon and Dee arrived at the cabin, U was waiting for them on the porch, while music was playing from his car. He stepped down from the porch and greeted them warmly. Then they began to unload the vehicle, placing some things inside the cabin and others in the truck that Ross had left on the property. After the supplies had all been put in their appropriate places, they sat on the porch and rested.

After a short break, Solomon drew in a deep breath and announced that it was time. He grabbed a wheelbarrow filled with tools and U grabbed more tools. Solomon paused near the two trees his father had planted so long ago, and Dee held his hand. "This will be the last time we do the ritual honoring the ancestors," her dad said. After they performed the final ritual together, her dad took a roll of string from the wheelbarrow and tied a bow around each tree. He told U that he would make the first cut on each tree, then he would cut down the father tree, and U would cut the mother tree.

Dee sat and watched for a while as the men worked, but she quickly grew bored and ran off to follow a butterfly that flew past her face. She followed it for a distance and didn't realize how far she had gone. Dee could hear water nearby from the stream, and lay down to rest for a moment. She closed her eyes and took a deep breath full of scents from the woods and stream. She loved being in nature and was at peace.

When she opened her eyes, her body was levitating above the grass. It felt good, so she closed her eyes again and fell into a light sleep. In this state, she could see her dad and Uncle U in her mind's eye. Both men were sweating as they worked hard chopping down the trees. She felt and saw her dad's sadness, both in his face and in his thoughts as he cut the father tree.

Some time had passed, and Solomon took a break to look around for Dee. When he didn't see her, he called out for her, and Dee floated back down and ran to him. He was on one knee with his hands outstretched, so she ran and jumped to hit his hands then ran circles around him. He smiled at her playfulness and said, "It's time for lunch, Little D." Then U asked if he could finish cutting down the father tree because he was almost done with the mother. Solomon was older than U and seemed very tired, so he happily agreed, and U said, "It'd only be right that you take the final swings on both trees to bring them down." Solomon was grateful that U was there to help, and also impressed that he understood the significance of the trees.

Once he was rested, Solomon returned to the task of cutting down his beloved trees. He and U worked in silence until both trees fell. They then cut them into smaller pieces and loaded them onto the truck. The next day they took the truck loaded with the wood to a nearby farm. The farmer was known to make beautiful wood carvings and furniture, and Solomon said the man must have magical hands to make such beautiful creations.

They arrived at the farmer's barn, and Dee saw that it was full of art and unfinished furniture. She and Uncle U walked around looking at the many sculptures in the barn, as the farmer's men unloaded the wood from the truck. Solomon was in conversation when the farmer noticed U and Dee exploring. "There are horses in the back if you want to see them," he said. So Dee and U wandered off.

They spotted the horses and U sat Dee on top of the wooden fence so she could have a closer look. The horses neighed and walked toward her. U became nervous and stiffened up. Dee noticed his discomfort and advised him to think about something else when he felt tense. She stroked a black horse's head as it stood in front of her. Then a second black horse tried to come over to her but a brown horse pushed its way through, and she touched its head too. All the horses bowed their heads to Dee before they walked away. She looked back to see Uncle U raising his eyebrow at the demonstration. He lifted her down from the fence and returned to see Solomon waiting for them by the truck. U mentioned Dee's comfort with the animals and their reaction to her. "She has always had a way with animals," commented Solomon.

The following morning, Solomon received a frantic call from the farmer. He was babbling, and it was hard for her dad to understand. Finally, Solomon was able to determine that the farmer wanted him to come to his farm right away because he had something to show him. "Did something happen to the wood?" Solomon asked. The farmer assured him the wood was fine, and he was calling about something else entirely. U left to return home, while Dee and Solomon headed back to the farm.

The farmer was waiting at the gate when they arrived. Once in the barn, he gave her dad a piece of wood. Solomon's eyes began to fill with tears, and he showed it to Dee. It was an image of two people holding hands. She had no idea what it meant to her dad, but she knew it made him happy. The farmer then gave her dad a second piece of wood, and this one evoked a deep emotional response from him as well. On that piece of wood, there was an image of a man and a child standing between two trees.

"Has anyone else seen these?" Solomon asked.

"No, no one has," the farmer replied. "These are the last two pieces I cut from the trees to make your chair."

"Well, they are very special to me, and I will display them on the wall at my cabin," Solomon said as he thanked the farmer for calling him.

On their way back to the cabin, Solomon explained the images to Dee. "The piece with the two adults holding hands are my parents," he said. "The second piece with the man and child—that's you and me." They smiled in amazement all the way back to the cabin.

The chair was ready a few days later, and they returned with the truck to pick it up. The farmer tried to engage her dad in small talk, but he was far too anxious to see the chair. He followed the farmer to the barn and examined the chair very closely, running his hands across every inch. The farmer had been concerned that the material Solomon had chosen would not be a good match, but the chair was perfect. Solomon sat in the chair and closed his eyes and smiled. Dee used her abilities and knew that he was seeing a vision of his mother and father. He leaned back in the chair, and the farmer walked away saying he would be right back.

Her father kept his eyes closed without responding. Dee continued watching him but had to interrupt because the farmer stopped short when he returned and stared at Solomon strangely. Dee called out to wake him up, and he opened his eyes and slowly rose from his new chair.

"Are the other items ready for pick-up?" he asked.

"Yes, they are," replied the farmer.

"Good. I will send you something extra for the two pieces of wood you gave me," said Solomon.

"Do you have them with you?" the farmer asked. "I can treat and protect them, and it will only take an hour to finish."

Solomon had the wood with him in the truck and agreed to let the farmer treat them.

While the farmer was preserving the wood, Solomon and Dee walked around his farm, coming to rest in a pasture to sit in the sun together. The men loaded the chair and other items of furniture onto the truck, and they headed back to the cabin. Once they arrived, Solomon unloaded the pieces that were to remain in the cabin, and they returned back home with the rest the next day.

When they arrived home, Ella told Solomon to wait for the older boys to get home so they could unload the truck for him. Later that evening while at dinner, Solomon announced that no one except Dee and himself were to sit in his new chair, and no one seemed to care.

Over the next couple of days, Dee made a pillow for his chair. She placed some magical items inside it that she had got from the Shaman's home and set her mind on what she wanted the items to do. They were to help her dad relax and to keep the half-siblings away from the chair. When the pillow was finished, she raced to present it to her dad who was sitting in his new chair. He lifted her over his head as he leaned forward to allow her to place the pillow behind his back. Dee didn't tell him about the magical items inside.

One day while her dad was gone, Alex decided that he wanted to try out Solomon's new chair, even though he had been told not to sit in it. As soon as he sat, he shot up as though something was wrong. The other siblings saw his reaction and asked what happened. "I don't know!" Alex replied. "Something shocked me. I hate that chair, and I'll never sit in it again!" From that point on, his other siblings avoided the chair at all costs, fearing that they would be shocked too.

Challenges: Red Balls

During another trip to the cabin, Solomon taught Dee a new game to play. Dee, U and Solomon walked to the nearby stream to gather some rocks that rested at the bottom. A red substance covered them, and her dad used another rock to scrape it off. Then he put the substance in a big piece of tree bark and added a little dirt, and squeezed it together until it looked like red clay. "You're going to make small balls with this and throw them at as many trees as you can in three minutes," Solomon said.

"Are you preparing her for an event?" U asked.

"Watch, and let's see how she does first," was the reply.

The two men backed away from the area where Dee would begin. "I'll tell you when to start, and you can physically throw the balls at the trees, run to them or use your powers," said her dad. She looked at Uncle U with uncertainty, as she rarely displayed her abilities in front of anyone but her dad. Solomon saw her hesitation and reassured her. "Uncle U is okay," he advised. "Don't worry, just focus on the task."

Dee walked over to where there were many trees and ran a big circle around several of them. She sat on the ground and began making small balls of clay and waited for her dad. Solomon clicked a stopwatch and told her to begin. She stayed seated on the ground, closed her eyes, and performed her magick.

"Dee doesn't understand what to do," said U.

"Just look at the clay and her hands," said Solomon.

The red clay balls were flying away from her hands and landing hard against several trees, making perfect circles. Before her time was up, she had already run out of clay balls and was waiting on her dad.

She looked back and saw U stumble backward, seemingly afraid of what he just witnessed. She stayed put, not wanting to cause further anxiety. It was the first time she had ever seen U that way. Solomon tried to ease his shock. "Come help me count the red marks on the trees," he said. After a moment of hesitation, U agreed, and Dee remained seated. She knew they were talking about her, but she couldn't make out the words. As they emerged from the thicket, U was smiling and patting her dad on the back.

"That's beautiful about your daughter, man. It's out of this world," he stammered. "She's better than I was," Solomon proudly said.

A New Trip:

A few days later, Solomon and Dee set out on another trip. They went to an airport and took a short flight to a location unknown to Dee. A man named Raul greeted Solomon upon arrival and took them to see the man in charge at a training facility not far away.

Once inside, Dee saw that the building looked like a huge gymnasium. Many people were occupied with various activities, separated into groups. Some were doing martial arts, exercising or sitting cross-legged meditating. As the group walked through the area, a tall white man in a military jumpsuit approached and greeted Solomon. They acknowledged each other as though they were acquaintances. "Is this the young child who hit so many trees?" he asked. "Yes, this is my daughter," Solomon replied. After a short conversation, the man in the jumpsuit told them where they would be staying until the event started that evening.

Raul escorted them to their accommodation, and once they had settled in, Dee went to wash up, and Solomon and U began talking.

"Time for a nap," Solomon said to Dee when she came out of the bathroom.

"It's still early; why can't I stay up?" Dee asked.

"You need to get some rest before the event this evening," her dad replied.

Dee lay down to rest, and Solomon and U stayed up late into the evening. Several hours later, Dee woke up hearing a loud buzzing noise throughout the hotel. She jumped out of bed and ran to her dad who was still engaged in a conversation with U. "It's a warning that the event's going to start soon," he explained. "Go wash up so you can eat something before we leave." By the time Dee had finished washing up; her dad had ordered some fruit and vegetables for her. Dee saw her competition outfit on her bed. It was a black jumpsuit with a red stripe on one leg and one arm. "These are the colors I wore when I participated in this event long ago," her dad said. "Now everyone will know who you are representing." Dee could see her dads' energy bristling excitedly around him and knew this was an important challenge to him.

They quickly arrived at the destination where the event would take place and drove up a large hill. They saw a huge brightly lit obstacle course deep in the bottom of a valley. There were wheelbarrows, wooden walls with ropes, ponds, trees and small windowless buildings. Military trucks filled with men wearing green military uniforms pulled into the course. They all got out of the trucks and took positions behind trees, while others stood out in the open. U observed, "The soldiers have an easy job. All they have to do is avoid getting hit by the balls."

"That's true, and those who don't get hit are handsomely rewarded, so they all look forward to coming to this event every year," Solomon said. "Some of them have been participating for years and are quite good at evading the balls."

"What happens to the men that get hit by the balls?" U asked.

"They exit the course through the small buildings," he replied.

Solomon retrieved a bag containing small balls filled with a red substance. "You have to hit as many of the men in the green army uniforms as you can, just as you did with the trees at the cabin," he said. He whispered in her ear, "There are no rules." Solomon and U accompanied Dee to the beginning of the course. She saw other participants at a distance wearing different colors, but even from afar she could tell they were all much older than her, in fact, she was the only child around. Her balls were the color of her red stripe, and the closest participant to her had on a white jumpsuit with a yellow stripe, and his balls were yellow.

Some of the army men laughed when they saw Dee. "She is just a little girl. Why is she participating in this event? What can she do?" Without responding to the men, Solomon got on one knee. "Focus on the task, not the men, and then you will have the last laugh," he said with a smile. High on a tower was a man holding a flag, about to signal the start of the event. Before backing away, Solomon told Dee a final time to focus on the task. The flag was dropped and the lights shut off, darkening the whole area inside the valley.

Dee picked up her bag of balls and calmly walked over to the closest wheelbarrow. She could see the energy of the soldiers standing in the open, while others tried to hide. Some of the participants rushed onto the course and began chasing the men, but Dee stayed put. She emptied the red balls onto the ground, and raised her arms and closed her eyes to use her magick. The balls were floating in front of her, and she made them swirl in the air in the form of a circle. Dee made sure the balls would not hurt the men by going all the way through their bodies.

Then she took a deep breath and blew on the balls, and they all flew across the field hitting all the men in her area three times. Out of balls, Dee remained behind the wheelbarrow until the event was over. As she waited, she could hear some of the army men complaining about being hit by her balls. The lights came back on, and she ran over to her dad and U. Some of the men that had been hit by her balls began walking toward them. U saw them approaching and put his hand on his gun as he stepped in front of Dee and Solomon.

One of the soldiers demanded to know how she cheated. "You're just a little girl, and there's no way you could have hit so many men with your balls without cheating!"

"How dare you insult her that way!" U snapped. "We will make sure that this is the last time you participate in this event." He removed his hand from his gun and started to write the names displayed on the soldiers' uniforms.

Another soldier quickly apologized. "We didn't mean to accuse anyone of cheating, but I've been participating in this event for a long time and have never been hit once. How was this little girl able to hit so many men three times each?" he asked.

"Well, you can take that up with your commander and the coordinators," Solomon replied. "You can't cheat if there are no rules."

Some of the soldiers walked away but continued to complain. Then another soldier suggested they all leave the course before they got into trouble. "Don't worry about them; their pride is just hurt because they are grown men," Solomon advised U. "To get taken down by a little girl is a blow to their manhood, especially as some of them have been coming to this event since they were young recruits."

Soon the buzzer sounded, and all the men came back on the course to be counted. The soldiers stood in formation as men in white coats walked through each row. The men carried a metal box that had an orange stick protruding from it. They would move the device over the soldiers' uniforms, and the orange stick would blink and count the marks. The soldiers were still whispering to each other and looking over at Dee.

After all the hits had been counted, a man walked over to Solomon, who was holding Dee in his arms. "There's no need to count further," he said. "You've obviously won. Congratulations." The man asked Solomon to follow him to the podium where others were waiting to congratulate them on the victory. Solomon asked U to hold Dee while he met with them. Then one of the men said, "Bring the little girl with you so we can congratulate her as well."

Solomon lost his smile and said, "My daughter is not to be approached." All the men looked at her, and she felt their negative energies. She turned her head into Uncle U's chest to avoid looking their way. After a short silence, one of the men said, "We will honor your wishes as you are her father and have participated in this event before."

Then, an old man with gray hair and beard said, "I would like to see her go through the course again, this time with the lights on. To witness such a spectacle would be a marvelous wonder." Solomon replied, "Yes, it would be, but we have already won and will not be repeating the event ever again." The old man then wrote something in Solomon's journal and asked him to step near a wall so a photo could be taken.

Some of the previous winners of the event had photos on the wall, and Solomon agreed to have a photo taken of him, but not of Dee. One of the men called for the carver, who climbed a ladder and chipped away at the wall. He was told to put Solomon and Dee's names on the top and to leave lots of space so that they could be seen clearly and separate from the others. "No one has ever hit so many men and certainly not three times each. We must remember what happened here today," he said excitedly.

U said, "Take a look at your dad over there. That's the look of a very proud father." Dee looked at her father closer with her second sight and saw that his energy was indeed glowing brighter than usual. He seemed to enjoy this event more than he let on.

The army men started chanting, "Red, Red, Red!" Solomon motioned for U to let Dee come over to him. U kept her in his arms and handed her to her father. Solomon kissed his daughter on her cheek and held her tightly. Dee could tell her dad was very happy, so she embraced his powerful energy, and it felt good. She didn't understand why the people continued to say "Red" and asked her dad what it meant.

"They're chanting it because we won!" he exclaimed. "Black and red are the colors you wore during the event and the colors of our true inner being."

Dee looked at the wall and saw the carved names of people from all over the world, and she and Solomon's names stood out from all of them. When they left the event, she could see that the glow around her dad remained. "I can't wait to see you in action again, Little D," U said happily.

Challenges: Fire Walking

Solomon was preparing to take a trip to the mountains for a gathering. He called Dee over to him. "We're going to an event, and I was told that there would be other children. Do you want to come along?" Dee screamed, "Yes, I want to go!" She jumped up and down in excitement. Ella packed their bags, food and a special drink that the Shaman recommended Dee drink daily, and they were off.

Solomon, Dee, and U boarded a plane that had a few other families as fellow passengers. Some had cameras around their necks and wore brightly colored tropical style shirts and safari hats. Everyone seemed to be having a good time, but traveling with other people was unusual for Dee and Solomon. They would typically travel alone or sometimes with one or two other government men who would hitch a ride.

The plane landed, and when they disembarked, a man was waiting for them in front of a car. U loaded their bags in the trunk, and they drove until they had to switch vehicles to one more suited for the trek up the mountain. The 4x4 utility vehicle handled the twisty narrow roads with ease and brought them to their destination at the top. There were small log cabins scattered about that made for a rustic appearance in the mountain retreat. Some people were busy laying coals between large river rocks on either side. Solomon said it would be used for the eclipse ritual to be performed later on that evening.

The trio settled inside one of the cabins and then walked around the retreat and saw that they were the only people of color at the event. Dee noticed some children playing in a picnic area, and two blonde-haired girls with white dresses on ran towards her but stopped before reaching her. "Can I go play?" Dee asked. "Sure you can," her dad replied. So Dee ran to the girls as they took her hands and skipped toward the other women and children sitting at the picnic tables. She looked back and could see that Solomon and U had sat down while keeping an eye on her. The kids were eating hot dogs, so Dee took a carrot she had in her pocket and started to munch on it. A woman saw her and offered her a hot dog instead. Dee politely declined. The other children watched her eat the carrot with curious looks on their faces. Then the two girls and Dee ran off to play, and some of the other children joined in.

After Dee had played with the children for quite a while, it was time for the event. The burning hot fire trail glowed in the night, and everyone gathered around the leader of the ceremony.[12] The children and most of the women remained at the distant picnic area. Dee waved goodbye to her playmates before running over to her dad and U, who remained seated. She wanted to witness the fire ritual. The leader spoke of the importance of the eclipse occurring that evening and of the fire walking ritual that was about to take place. Four men would walk over the burning coals, and they were all dressed in shiny silver shirts and pants.

The first man stepped onto the beginning of the trail and stood to watch the crowd around him for a few moments before turning away in defeat. The heat was too much for him, and he gave up before he even set foot on the surface. The second man did the same. The third man stepped on the coals but only took a few steps before leaping off, unable to go any further. The fourth man was much more determined to complete the ritual. He made it halfway across before falling to his hands and knees. He was lifted from the coals, but not before sustaining severe burns to his feet, hands, and knees. They took him away to have his wounds attended to, and no one else stepped forward.

Dee was about five years old and watched the burning coals for a while. She whispered to her father, "I can walk on the hot trail. Let me do it!" Solomon thought about it for a moment. "Are you sure, Little D?" he asked. "That trail is very hot." Dee, inherently a warrior, said, "Yes, I'm sure." Solomon approached the group's leader and asked to speak to him. "My daughter wants to walk the trail," he advised, as Dee held his hand. The leader looked at him incredulously and laughed. "She's a little girl."

"She will be just fine. Will you allow it?" Solomon asked.

"Absolutely not," he replied. "That's out of the question. We cannot be responsible for this young child if she is injured."

Seeing that the leader would not permit her to walk, Solomon produced a letter from his pocket he had received from a high-ranking Freemason that invited him to come. The leader examined the letter and conferred with two

---

[12] Fire walking is thousands of years old, with records dating back to Iron Age India in 1200 B.C. It was practiced by many religions as a rite of passage, a test of strength and courage, or, in religion, as a test of faith. (See h2g2.)

other men nearby. After a short discussion, the leader threw his hands in the air in resignation and gave his permission.

The leader called for a woman, and after a brief discussion, she approached Solomon and Dee with a silver suit in her hand. It was much too large, but another of the women in attendance went to her cabin and returned with scissors and tape. Solomon and U watched as they went to work cutting and taping the material so that Dee would be able to wear the makeshift outfit.

Solomon escorted Dee to the beginning of the trail and asked a final time if she was certain that she wanted to fire walk. "Yes, I'm sure," Dee replied without hesitation. Solomon released her hand and stepped back. Dee stood at the beginning staring at the hot trail as everyone watched in anticipation. She focused her attention on the trail, cooling it with her mind. After a while, she began the ritual walking at a slow pace—contrary to her dad's advice as he urged her to move faster. Dee continued her slow pace, maintaining the rhythm she had set for herself, and completed the entire walk to the amazement of the crowd that watched in stunned silence.

Solomon scooped her up and performed a perfunctory examination of her feet. There appeared to be no burns, but he took her to their cabin anyway for a better look. He cleaned the soot from her feet and saw only slight redness but not one true burn. Then he rubbed a solution he got from the Shaman on her feet as a precaution. U came into the cabin and told Solomon that the leader wanted to speak with him. They were all talking about Dee and couldn't figure out how the little girl was able to walk the fire trail, and not one adult could do it. "If they don't understand what they just saw, then they didn't deserve to witness it," said Solomon.

He sent Dee to bed, and U stayed with her while Solomon went to speak with the leader. Upon Solomon's return to the cabin, he told U that the leader wanted to keep Dee at the retreat to probe her. Solomon was outraged at the disrespect they had been shown. "When I return home, I will be in contact with the Supreme Leader who requested that we attend this gathering," he announced in annoyance. "I will voice my dissatisfaction to him."

The following morning as they were leaving, the leader of the gathering shouted out to Solomon as they got into the vehicle, "Leave the girl!" The other attendees watched the exchange between the men. Solomon approached the leader and said something that clearly offended the man because he had a strange look on his face but kept quiet. The trio left and drove away in the 4x4 vehicle.

On the flight back home, Solomon told U that he would be stopping to meet with the Supreme Freemason Leader to advise him of the incidents that had occurred over the last 24 hours. He encouraged U to go home, and they would meet again on the next trip.

Once they landed, Dee and her dad headed to their meeting with the Supreme Leader at a restaurant. Although the restaurant was almost empty, they were seated far in the back because they were black. The Supreme Leader arrived a short time later and immediately moved them to a table of his choosing. The leader listened as Solomon recounted the circumstances of the previous evening and that morning. The leader was surprised at Dee's accomplishment but also outraged and embarrassed at how they had been treated after the fact. He told Solomon that he would handle the situation personally.

"I stand by my word; nothing will be done by us to your special child," said the Supreme Freemason Leader. He wrote something in Solomon's journal and extended an invitation for them to dine with him. Solomon declined, explaining that he had to take his daughter back home after a long day.

Challenges: Dangerous Town

Solomon, U, and Dee continued their world travels fulfilling the requirements necessary to gain Dee's admittance into the mystery schools. On one such occasion, they left the country to a destination known for its unsavory inhabitants. Everyone carried weapons, and it wasn't out of the norm for somebody to be killed in the streets. The only rule was that there were no rules. Solomon and U had prepared themselves for the trip, but they had also arranged to meet someone in town to assist with hiring a security detail. Although Solomon had U along, he knew it was truly Dee who protected them.

The group arrived at a small airport and was met by their escort. He looked surprised and stared at the group, and when he finally spoke, his English was broken. "Sorry, mister, for staring, but you really looks funny and stands out. It's not often we see two black men with little girl in this country. The town you go to is very dangerous place, you need escorts."

"I know. Are there escorts in place for us?" Solomon asked.

"They at the bar waiting to discuss deal for services," the driver answered.

As they drove away in the escort's truck, it seemed as though they were passing through a war-torn area. The town was in a shambles, dilapidated buildings were everywhere. Men and women walked around with rifles, and the bar they went to was in no better shape than the other buildings. When they entered, they saw six men drinking together at a table. The escort spoke to one of the men at the table, made the introductions and left to wait outside.

The man who would negotiate with Solomon for the security detail also spoke some English and invited him to sit at a booth in the far corner of the bar. U and Dee stood by the door to watch. Solomon and the man spoke for a few minutes, and Dee noticed her dad handing him a jewel, presumably as payment for services. Then Solomon got up and strolled over to join U and Dee by the door. The man took the stone to the table for his companions to examine. Dee could hear them speaking, and heard one say, "We should take the jewel and dispose of them." She was about to inform her dad of what she had heard, but the man Solomon had spoken with was approaching. "You should be on your way now, or you will die where you stand," he insisted.

Solomon looked to U, who was about to draw his weapon and said, "Stand firm." Dee sensed what was happening as well as what was about to happen. She squeezed her dad's hand, and he looked down at her. It was his way of letting her know she could do what she needed to protect them. She raised her hand and looked away from her dad. The other men got up, and one of them pointed a gun at U. Reading the energy in his hand, she knew he was about to pull the trigger . . . And he did.

Using her gifts, Dee stopped the bullet from hitting U. She then caused all the men to stop breathing by pulling the air from their lungs. The men were now utterly confused and dropped their weapons. They tried to regroup and reach for their guns, but fell to the floor choking on their own fluids. A few moments later, all the men lay motionless on the floor, dead. At only five years old, Dee was saddened that she had had to take such extreme measures to protect herself, U and especially her dad. Solomon saw how upset Dee was and lifted her up in his arms to comfort her.

"I feel bad for ending the mean men. Why did they make me do it?" she asked.

"Don't let it bother you Little D," her dad advised. "They were not honorable good men, and they were going to rob and kill us." Reassured by her father's words, she immediately let the sadness float away.

"Get the jewel from the guy's pocket," Solomon told U before they left the bar.

The driver was outside and seemed surprised that they all came out intact. He walked into the bar and saw that all six men lay dead on the floor. He seemed both astounded and confused as he examined the bodies. "How did you do this with such dangerous men?" he asked. "There are no gunshot wounds or trauma to their bodies."

"Just do your job and get us decent escorts," was Solomon's only reply.

"Yes, sir. You shall not have any more problems," said the driver.

The driver went back into the bar to examine the dead men again. He retrieved their guns and began rifling through their pockets. Then he took them to meet another crew that could provide security.

They drove for a while before arriving at a building. "You're welcome to come inside with me," said the driver. As they all were exiting the vehicle, a man emerged from the building and immediately shook Solomon's hand. This man used proper English as he spoke. "I heard about what had happened to the other crew. Those men were untrustworthy murderers, and they deserved what they got," he said brusquely. "But how did you do it?" he asked.

Solomon ignored the man's question and got right to the point. "I'm here to discuss a deal for a security detail." He showed the man the jewel that would be the payment for services. The man scrutinized the jewel and stuck it in his pocket, and an agreement was made. "Whatever you need while you're in town, we will be more than happy to help," said the man. He was still perplexed as to how only one shot was fired, and six men died without bruises or cuts. "Word travels quickly in this town, and everyone knows what happened. There will be no further trouble for you," he advised.

The occupants of the town were all talking about the two black men with the little girl who had eliminated a notorious group of killers. All now feared the trio and their visit to the country would never be forgotten.

The full memory of this trip has not been fully recovered by Dee.

Missing Son

Solomon received a call from someone requesting a favor. After hanging up, he grabbed a chair and sat next to Dee. "I'm going on a little trip, but you're not coming with me this time," he said. "I will be traveling with a few men to arrange a meeting, and I want you to stay at home and not leave the front yard." Dee nodded and said, "Okay." Solomon turned to leave, but then snapped his fingers as if he forgot something. He turned on his heel down the hallway, and Dee followed him to his room. Her father pulled out the black pouch he carried around his neck and laid it on the bed.

When Solomon had left, Dee examined the contents of the pouch. They were items the Shaman had given him for protection. As she dug around inside the pouch, something pierced her skin. Suddenly everything went dark, and the air was sucked from her lungs. It only took a moment for the air to return, and it felt like the dawn of a new day as her vision returned.

Dee found herself standing in an unfamiliar front yard as images began appearing before her eyes. She saw a mailbox, dry brown grass and an old house with a rocking chair on the front porch. She could hear a boy in the back yard say, "My dad is going to put you in jail forever!" Then she heard a man's laughing voice responding, "Your dad couldn't even find the jail without help."

Dee moved to the side of the house where she could see what was happening more clearly. The man had the young boy in a tight hold. The boy bit his arm in an attempt to escape. "Damn you!" the man screamed, before punching the boy and his body went limp. The unconscious boy was dragged to a storm cellar, and the man locked the door with a padlock before going into the house. Dee went to the cellar door and shook the lock to see if she could open it. The noise attracted the man's attention, and he came back out to check the door. Dee noticed a radio in his hands as he looked around the property before driving away. With that, Dee was back in Solomon's bedroom. She opened her eyes and saw her mom and dad watching over her.

"I knew something was going to happen on this trip," said her mom.

"I need to speak with her alone," said her dad.

When her mom left the room, Dee recounted her experience to her dad, and afterward, he decided to take her along after all. Ella was infuriated when Solomon told her Dee was going along. She thought it was absolutely wrong for her five-year-old daughter to accompany her husband on his trips. She wanted Dee to stay home with her other children. As her mom and dad were arguing, Dee heard Solomon say, "I've already explained it to you before, and I'll repeat it for the millionth time: Dee is not like your other children, or like any child for that matter."

Solomon and Dee left very early the next morning and met up with the rest of the traveling party. Besides them, there were four others: two white men and two younger black men. One of the white men couldn't understand why Solomon had brought a child along with him.

"You should drop the child off at home before we leave," he said.

"Don't concern yourself with my daughter," replied Solomon. "She will be coming along so let's just get this over with."

That being settled, they drove for a while, until one of the men said they were approaching the Mississippi state line. In Mississippi, police were known for their cruel and unfair treatment of black people. One of the black men who had been sleeping wiped his eyes and looked out the window as if he was on high alert.

After passing a large green sign, Dee told her dad, "The men with badges are going to stop us near a big blue metal tank." The driver seemed distracted by what she had said and veered out of his lane.

"Watch the road," said Solomon.

"What did she mean by 'men with badges'? Who is she talking about?" he asked. Solomon made a motion with his hand waving the question off without saying a word.

It was still very early in the morning, and not many vehicles were on the road. One of the passengers in the back seat spotted a police car ahead of them hiding behind an advertising sign.

"They're coming for us," said Solomon before they even passed the car.

"I'm not driving over the speed limit, so why would they stop us?" the driver asked.

Then Dee pointed ahead to a large blue metal tank. The police car sped up behind them with sirens on, and the driver pulled over.

"How did she know we would be pulled over by this tank?" he asked.

"Pay attention to the situation at hand and don't worry about my daughter," Solomon replied.

Two policemen approached the car, weapons drawn. One went to the driver's side, the other to the passenger's side. They ordered the group to put their hands in the air. Dee was on her dad's lap and stuck her head and arms out the window. With weapons still pointed at them, the police opened the doors and ordered Solomon and the other two black passengers to step behind the vehicle. The two white men were instructed to go to the front of the vehicle.

While one officer questioned the white men, the other stood guard over Dee, Solomon and the two black men at the back of the car, checking their identifications. The officer instructed Dee to step away from her dad and come to him, but she refused and clung to her dad's leg all the more. He still had his gun drawn, and Solomon advised him to put it away because it was upsetting his daughter and they were not a threat to him. The officer holstered his gun and looked down at Dee. She noticed a familiar look about him and also noticed that his pupils changed from round to oval. He backed away from her as if something he had seen in her terrified him, or maybe she had seen something that exposed him.

The officer at the front of the vehicle walked to the patrol car and used the radio to call for a transport vehicle. The second officer approached his partner and said, "I don't want that little girl in my car; she is frightening."

"Relax, that's not happening," his partner said. "Joe is bringing a transport vehicle to pick up the niggers, and we will be transporting the two white men. But don't think for a second that I'm not telling the boys back at the station that you're afraid of a little nigger girl."

The second officer remained adamant. "There's something about her that just isn't right."

"Tell that to Joe when he arrives," his partner said sarcastically.

Officer Joe arrived on the scene with the transport vehicle, and Dee, Solomon and the two black men were told to get inside. The two white men got into the other police car. One of the black men said nervously, "I heard that the police in Mississippi take black people to the woods and kill them." Solomon replied, "We will be just fine and on our way before nightfall." The men trusted what Solomon said. Then the officer returned to the car, and they all drove away together.

They were transported to the police station, and it became clear that the town was segregated. Many white people stopped and stared at the group as if they were watching a parade. The vehicles pulled up in front of a police station that had two white pillars in front. An American and a Confederate flag hung from poles at the top of the building. Two policemen approached the vehicles to help with escorting Solomon and the men inside. As the group got out of the car, a fat white man in overalls and a red shirt sauntered up to the vehicle with a rifle in his hand.

"Do you need help with the niggers?" he asked.

"You best go home before I arrest you for carrying that rifle around town," said one of the officers.

Once inside the police station, Dee saw a photo of the boy she'd had a vision of posted on the walls. She also heard someone talking about a missing boy. She quietly let her dad know that it was the same boy she had seen in her vision. Her dad acknowledged this as they were escorted down the hall to the cells. An officer held his hand out for Dee, but she quickly withdrew behind her dad. "My daughter will be staying with me at all times," said Solomon. The officer ignored him and knelt down so that he could look at her. Then he tried coaxing her into the other room with promises of candy and cookies. But Dee turned away and continued to cling to her father's leg. A female officer approached her with the cookies and candy to show her they really did have them.

"She doesn't eat such things. What are we being held for anyway?" Solomon demanded.

"All kids like candy," said the female officer, ignoring Solomon's question.

"That doesn't answer my question. What are we being held for?" Solomon asked again. "I would like to know so I can make my phone call."

"We can't have a child in our jail, and there are no charges on you, but one of the other black men you were traveling with has an outstanding warrant from another state. So we will be keeping you here until that is cleared up," she said.

Solomon knew that Dee had seen the missing boy in her visions and wanted to help find him before it was too late. He kneeled down and whispered to her, "We should help find that boy. Do you know if he is okay?"

Dee nodded. "He's okay."

"Can you find him?"

"The directions are easy," said Dee. "It's the first turn past the blue tank where we got stopped. To the right will be an old house and that's where the boy is"

Solomon stood up and announced, "I will try to help find the missing boy, and in exchange, all the men in our traveling party will be released." One of the officers went to the police chief's office to relay the message, and Solomon asked to use the phone. He made his phone call, all while holding Dee on his lap. The female officer was sitting in the chair next to them, and Dee turned towards her dad and held onto him with both arms so the officer wouldn't try and reach for her again.

After the conversation, Solomon put the phone down and told the officer to transfer the call to the police chief. The officer gave Solomon a disgruntled look before going to the police chief's office. The police chief began yelling at the female officer in his office, drawing a crowd into the room. Then the police chief approached Solomon. "I spoke to someone who advised me that you can assist us," he said. "I don't know how, but you better be telling the truth about helping us find that boy, or you will never leave the state of Mississippi," he added in a threatening voice.

Then four white men in black suits barged into the office before Solomon could reply. Dee placed her hands over her ears because she sensed that one of the men would yell at her dad and demand to know where his son was, which was exactly what happened. But before Solomon could utter a word, two women rushed in demanding the same. One of the women was the boy's mother. She approached Solomon and raised her hand to strike him. Seeing this, Dee swiftly placed her cheek on her dad's cheek.

The woman backed off and ran into the arms of the older woman she was with.

Solomon stood up. "We need to find the boy immediately," he said.

"I have to check something at my house; I need a little time off," said the officer with the oval eyes.

"No one is going anywhere until my son is found," said the boy's father.

Solomon and Dee were escorted to a black sedan that belonged to the boy's father. He spoke to his wife for a moment before getting into the car. While in the car alone with Solomon and Dee, he asked, "Is my son still alive? Please tell me."

"He is," Solomon replied. "But I don't know whether he is injured or not."

"I received a call on your behalf and was told that you possess psychic gifts and can help find my boy," said the father.

"I didn't know he was missing until I saw his pictures at the station today," said Solomon. "If you can, have one of your security men question the officer who requested leave to go home. I have a feeling he knows something about your boy."

The boy's father was an elected official, and one of his men called the cop with the oval eyes to the car and questioned him. "Have you ever seen Solomon or any of his traveling companions before and do you know anything about the missing boy?" he asked bluntly.

"I've never seen these people before until I stopped them on the road," the officer replied. "Why am I being questioned about the missing boy?"

"Because that boy is the son of _____, and as such, everyone, even the police chief, will be pulled in for questioning if necessary," the security man replied.

The officer went back to his patrol car without saying another word. The boy's father sat in the front seat with his driver, while Dee and her dad were in the back. Solomon relayed directions to the driver that Dee had given, and they sped away with several other police cars following. The boy's father looked at Dee with sadness in his eyes and asked, "Is your dad good to you?" Without responding to the man, Dee hugged Solomon and whispered, "I love you, Dad." Solomon squeezed her in his arms and whispered that he loved her also. "She doesn't speak to strangers," said her dad.

The car sped past the blue tank. It took the first exit and turned right at the fork in the road. An officer on the radio said, "You're going the wrong way! That property belongs to me." They continued on, ignoring the officer. Soon they arrived at the house. The men in suits, along with the officers, were scrambling about the property. "Find the storm cellar; that's where the boy is!" yelled Solomon.

The officer who owned the property came barreling into the backyard with his patrol car. "You better get everyone off my property unless you have a search warrant!" he threatened. In reply, the boy's father punched him in the face, knocking the officer to the ground. Before the officer could get up to retaliate, another officer came out of the storm cellar with the missing boy. "I got him, and he's okay! the officer shouted.

The officer with the oval eyes was restrained with handcuffs as the boy's father ran to his son and held him in his arms. "Tell my wife that our son has been rescued and take me to the nearest hospital." During the drive to the hospital, the man held his son and stroked his head repeating over and over, "I love you, Teddy." Dee climbed on Solomon's lap trying to see the boy's face. She touched the boy's arm and said, "He will be okay."

The boy's father looked back at Dee and Solomon and thanked them. He handed Solomon a business card. "If there's ever anything I can do to help you, please call the number on this card. You only need to say the name Teddy and give the number 361713, and you shall receive help."

When they arrived at the hospital, the father got out and placed his son on a gurney. His wife, who had just arrived, began showering her son with kisses. The driver drove Solomon and Dee back to the police station, and the rest of their party were released.

Challenges: The Crystal Key and the Labyrinth

Dee was in the front yard playing on a tricycle when her dad arrived one evening. He smiled as he picked her up and said, "We're going on another trip this evening to a place where there will be others that are special and gifted." He held her tightly in his arms and took a deep breath before continuing. "It will be one of the final tests 'they' require to prove your worthiness to attend the mystery schools. There will be many challenges ahead of you, Little D, so face them with courage." At around five years old, Dee had no idea what her dad meant by "worthiness," but she promised that she would do her best.

Ella entered the room and saw her daughter in her husband's arms. "Get down so your dad can get some rest before you all leave!" she yelled.

"There's no need to yell at her, Ella," Solomon responded. "I'll get some rest a little later, but right now I'm talking to her."

Ella seemed angry and screamed again. "Leave your dad alone and go play!"

Solomon didn't say a word. Instead, he sat Dee down on the couch and spoke to Ella discreetly. Afterwards, he went to his room to rest. Once Dee was alone, her mom approached with a disgusted look on her face. "You don't need to go with your dad; I can take you somewhere else. How about I take you, Emma, Fred and Deidre to the county fair to have fun?" Dee politely declined. "They don't play with me, and I'm going with dad because I have to take a test to prove my worthiness." She tried to explain to her mom the best she could. "Tell your dad you don't want to go, and that's settled!" said Ella while glaring at Dee.

Dee didn't want her mom to fuss at her anymore, so she sat in her room until her dad woke from his nap. She told him about the conversation she had with her mom.

"You don't have to go if you don't want to," her dad calmly explained.

"Of course I want to go," said Dee. "I just don't want Mom to be upset."

Her dad smiled. "Don't worry about your mom. The only reason she talks to you that way is because she has been speaking with people who believe it's not a good idea for a little girl to be traveling in the company of men. Your mom doesn't understand who you are or what you're capable of doing." He continued, "Some requirements need to be met to assure your successful entrance into the mystery schools. Those people she speaks with are trying to stop your development. People are often frightened by what they either cannot do or do not understand."

"What does 'suppress' mean?" Dee asked. "Mom always says that when she talks about me."

Solomon nodded. "It's when people prevent you from being who you really are by taking something away from you."

Dee understood what he meant, but it saddened her that Ella didn't want her to be who she truly was. She wondered what would happen if her mom ever got the chance to suppress her. It made her extra happy that her dad was around to protect her.

U was already in town visiting a friend and arrived later that evening to pick them up. Solomon kissed his wife on the cheek, in spite of her anger. Dee wanted to kiss her mom like her dad had just done and walked over to her. Ella lifted her daughter up and squeezed her so tightly in her arms that she couldn't breathe.

"It's good Dee decided to stay at home with me where she belongs!" Ella announced.

Dee could hardly get a breath but managed to scream out, "I'm going with my dad!"

Her mom put her back down hard, almost dropping her to the ground. She gave Solomon an angry look and walked back into the house. Solomon took Dee's hand and reassured her that everything would be fine and not to worry about her mom. As they drove away, Dee noticed Ella in the window watching them with the phone to her ear.

The group stopped in New Orleans on their way to an airport, because Solomon had business to take care of at the bank. "Wait here while I go inside. I'll be back in a few minutes," he said. Dee sat in the car with U as he flipped through the radio stations. True to his word, Solomon returned to the car minutes later. He had a manila envelope tucked under his arm that he put in his suitcase as he directed U to drive them to the airport.

Once at the airport, a private plane was standing by on the tarmac. Solomon instructed U to check his weapons, and since no one else was on board, he took the opportunity to strip his guns and clean them. The plane landed in an area where the weather was dark and gloomy. Dee felt that the place had incredibly low energy. They disembarked from the plane and met a fair-skinned man wearing a baseball cap. He drove them to their destination. The man's large truck rumbled down dirt roads, finally arriving at an industrial building that had the number 36 painted on the side, along with the letters "FDR" across the top.

"I'm not coming inside with you. Those men are dangerous," said the driver. "You should probably leave the girl outside too, lest she comes in harm's way."

Solomon instructed the man to stand by and be ready to leave when they returned. "My daughter will be coming with us," he said.

The warehouse had a few windows at the top and a metal platform at window level which wrapped around the perimeter of the building. There were twelve men armed with machine guns standing at the rail and one man near the entrance with a handgun similar to those that U carried.

The man near the entrance asked, "Who are you here to see?"

"We are here to make an exchange with Kufstein," replied Solomon.

"Leave the girl and go before you're all killed," the guard snapped back.

Solomon stated his business again, but this time with a warning. "You will not threaten us again, or you may find yourselves in grave danger."

The man did not take Solomon seriously. He laughed while pointing a gun at U's head. U then pointed his gun at the man's head. The men on the platform above turned and aimed their machine guns at them. "Stand firm," Solomon told U. He then demanded the guard retrieve Kufstein at once. He looked down at Dee briefly and then instructed the men to lower their weapons, or he would make them do so in his own way.

Considering that Solomon was outnumbered and outgunned, the guard didn't take his threat seriously. Dee sprang into action. She first turned her attention to the guard with the gun pointed at U. She sensed he was not going to pull the trigger, so she simply caused him to suffer extreme pain.

He began to shriek in agony. Next, she completely paralyzed the guards on the platform, forcing them to drop their weapons and fall to the floor. The guard with the handgun was screaming so loudly that the sound reverberated through the whole building. "I'm Kufstein's nephew! Please stop the torture," he begged. U kicked the gun away from him.

Two men came out of an upstairs office and looked down at them. It was impossible to mistake Solomon's anger as he addressed Kufstein. "I bring you what you need, and you greet me like this!" he exclaimed. "I should take the crystal key and burn these documents. You're dead without them." Kufstein looked at his men on the platform, and then at his nephew screaming in agony. He slowly walked down the steps. He extended his hand to Solomon as he apologized.

Solomon stepped back, refusing to shake his hand. "For the disrespect alone, I should kill your men and leave their bodies for the rats to feast on," said Solomon. Kufstein tried to inch closer to him, but U stepped in front and leveled his gun at his face. Kufstein begged for forgiveness. Solomon demanded he place the crystal key on the table. Kufstein did as instructed. U handed the key to Solomon, who then examined it for authenticity. Satisfied that it was the key, he took Dee's hand and stood before Kufstein. U grabbed Kufstein hard by the shoulders, digging his fingertips into pressure points and causing him to fall to his knees.

"If I ever see you or your nephew again, you're both dead," said Solomon.

As Solomon turned to leave, Kufstein pleaded, "Will you please leave the documents and release my men from whatever you have placed upon them?" Without a word, Solomon threw the envelope to the floor. He looked down at Dee, and she raised her hand high over her head, and all the men were relieved from their temporary state of trauma and paralysis. They all looked like lost and confused children instead of the dangerous guards they were supposed to be.

The driver was surprised to see the group back so quickly and unharmed. He commented on this to Solomon. U said, "Never mind that, getting us back to the landing strip is your only job." Once they arrived, Solomon instructed U to pay the man. "I've already been paid," said the driver. Disregarding him, U stuck an envelope in the driver's jacket pocket anyway. The driver thanked Solomon profusely as they boarded the plane.

Once on board and settled in, U said, "That was intense! I expected someone to get killed for sure." Solomon hunched his shoulders. "I guess Dee didn't sense it was necessary for anyone to lose their life and perhaps that's why they all lived." The two men continued talking about what had happened at the warehouse and what would be the next step of the journey. Dee still had no idea why the crystal key was so important or why the men had carried weapons. After all, she was only a child and not told very much.

Crystal Key

When the plane landed, Solomon instructed U to carry the bag with the crystal key while he carried Dee. He looked at his pocket watch and told U that they were running behind schedule. A driver was waiting for them as usual, and as they exited the airport, a guard stopped the car. He checked a piece of paper that was given to him by the driver and then walked around the car looking through the windows to verify the passengers. Once satisfied, he let them pass through, and they arrived at the dock without incident.

They boarded an empty boat, and the skipper arrived a short time later. "You people are on the wrong boat," he said. "This boat is a charter to the private island." The skipper was apparently expecting white passengers; it hadn't occurred to him that they could be black. "I've never transported a child or a black person to the island before," he said, once he realized they were the passengers he was expecting.

Solomon produced a black paper with a red dragon on it and held it up for the skipper to see. The skipper looked at the paper without touching it and ceased any further objections. "Do your job and save your words for others," said Solomon. "Your sole responsibility is to get us to the island." U stepped close to the skipper. "Be respectful, keep your mouth shut and do your job," he reiterated. Then they were finally on their way.

The wind felt refreshing on Dee's face, and the cool mist from the water felt soothing. She hung over the edge of the boat while her dad held her tightly so she could feel the splashes of water on her hands. She was eager to see some fish and closed her eyes for a moment. When she opened them again, many fish were swimming all around the boat. The skipper watched in amazement as the fish converged around his boat. He shouted, "Hey, what's going on? Where did all those fish come from?" U gave the man a serious look, and the skipper redirected his attention to steering the boat.

The boat arrived at the dock on the island where a deckhand was waiting to tie it up. The skipper offered to carry the bags, but U told him to stay put. The skipper scrunched up his face in annoyance but held his tongue. Once the bags were unloaded, the deckhand gave the skipper an envelope, untied the boat, and sent him on his way. It turned out that the deckhand was actually the leader at the compound, and he had personally come out to greet the trio. Without knowing what had occurred during the boat ride, he apologized for the skipper. "The boat captain can be very forward and nosey, but he's been with us for a while and gets the job done promptly," he said. "Let's get you to the compound and settled in."

They climbed into an electric vehicle, much like a golf cart, and drove across the grass past a few trees. Dee spotted a water fountain in the distance in the shape of an elephant, with water spouting from its trunk. Once they reached it, they parked their cart and had to walk a short distance until they reached some large archways. As they stepped through each archway, Dee sensed a change as if they were going through some sort of energy portal. Solomon also experienced a feeling come over him while going through the archways and mentioned it to U. Upon hearing Solomon's disclosure, the escort said, "Yes, this island is a very ancient and special place."

They passed the last archway and came to a small door surrounded by stones that led into a tunnel. The escort explained, "It will be dark when you enter, but the light will switch on within thirty seconds." Entry through that door was very restricted, but an exception was made for Solomon and U, as they were accompanying the first child to participate in the labyrinth event. Once inside U said, "You didn't exaggerate about the darkness, and it's very cool inside, almost like swimming in dark murky water without getting wet." The escort chuckled in agreement. "It's a typical reaction to the intense darkness."

They continued without saying another word until they reached the exit door. "There are lots of people on the other side," said Dee. Her dad acknowledged her remark by adjusting the luggage he was carrying on his shoulder and squeezing her tighter in his arms. As they walked through the door, they realized they were inside a huge coliseum. Dee looked up and could see a crowd of people on the bleachers above; some were sitting, some were walking around, while others looked down at the massive labyrinth.[13] Dee gripped her dad tighter as they walked towards a building.

A woman dressed in all yellow clothing approached them. Everything about her seemed to be the same shade of color, from her yellow shoes and clothes all the way up to her yellow hair. "She will show you to your accommodations," said the escort. "Then another woman will be visiting to ask for your color preference, and she will be responsible for preparing the child for the event." Before taking his leave he concluded, "We are all looking forward to seeing the outcome."

The lady in yellow led them into a building, and they walked through wide hallways full of people. The people were from many different countries, yet the trio remained the only black people and the only visitors with a child. The crowd stared at them, so U slowed down to speak with Solomon and suggested that they walk closer to the wall rather than in the middle of the hallway. Solomon agreed that it would be far less intrusive. They had fallen behind their guide, whose attention had remained straight ahead. She looked behind her and saw them near the wall and far behind. She waited for them to catch up and suggested they ignore the people. "They're just narrow-minded privileged rich people who don't fully understand who the child is or what will transpire tomorrow," she said. "Your room is not much further, only one more hallway and a staircase away. The whole floor has been reserved solely for you, and no one will be allowed on that level."

They reached the staircase and saw a large sign that read, "No guests allowed beyond this point." Solomon and Dee followed their guide past the sign and up the stairs. U had been trailing behind them but had momentarily stopped to keep his eye on a man who was rapidly approaching them.

"Hey, no one is permitted to go up the stairs," the man announced.

---

[13] A labyrinth is a complex structure that has only one entrance, which is also the exit. There is just one path from the entrance to the center. According to legend, it was built by Daedalus for King Minos of Crete at Knossos. Its function was to hold the minotaur, a creature with the head of a bull and the body of a man. Various labyrinth patterns have been found in North America, India, Scandinavia and Russia. In Christian tradition, labyrinths symbolize the complex and long path to God, ascension to salvation, or a pilgrimage to Jerusalem. In medieval times, a seven-circuit labyrinth was related to the planets, and a walk in the labyrinth was a cosmic journey through the heavens. The seven circuits can also represent the chakras, while the geometric shape of a labyrinth is believed to produce an energy field that can heal. Today, labyrinths are used for physical, mental, emotional, and spiritual experience by members of various belief groups.

"Keep moving and mind your own business," U retorted, without slowing his stride.

The man continued on his way and grumbled that he would be notifying someone about the occurrence.

They finally reached their room, and U entered first to check it out, and Solomon and Dee followed. Their guide stood by the door without entering and informed them that another woman would return to measure Dee and provide her with the appropriate clothing for the labyrinth event. The woman in yellow left and they all relaxed while waiting for the other woman to arrive. U expressed his concern about all the people that would be so close to Dee. Solomon assured him that they would be fine and no one would be near them once the event began.

An hour later there was a knock at the door. U checked with Solomon before opening the door. He allowed a man with a cart full of jumpsuits to enter the room. A woman who wore all red accompanied him. The red shade of her hair matched the outfit and shoes she wore. They seemed to be following a ritual of some kind that required people to wear one solid color, as they had seen many people dressed that way. The woman carried a clipboard and had a measuring tape draped over her shoulders. U and Solomon kept a close eye on Dee as she walked over to the cart filled with jumpsuits of different colors.

Dee used second sight to check the clothing for negative energy. The woman in red noticed her examining the different colors. "The materials have been touched by very few people," she advised. "They came directly from the maker to me." Dee continued to look through the suits and picked up a black suit that was next to a silver one. She scanned the glare coming from the sheen of the material, and the lady smiled and said, "Black is a fine choice." Dee hesitated for a second and decided to return the black suit to the cart and chose the silver one instead. After her selection, the woman said, "Many people have attempted to guess what color you would choose and all of them guessed wrong."

She stepped forward, removed the tape from her shoulders and reached out towards Dee. In an instant, Dee backed away and asked her dad to measure her. The lady explained that the measurements she needed to take would be fast and simple, requiring her only to wrap the tape around her enough times to measure her legs, waist, and arms. Solomon said he would do the measurements and quickly jotted them down for her.

The woman in red looked at the measurements and pulled several silver suits from the cart, finding the one that would fit Dee the best. She also gave her silver socks and shoes to match. Dee had noticed a long silver piece of cloth hanging from the side of the cart and asked if she might have it. The woman handed her the cloth and took the opportunity to say, "The labyrinth event is only held once every ten years, so it's an extraordinary time. If you so happen to navigate the sacred labyrinth successfully, you can choose a partner to accompany you to the mystery schools. The event will start promptly at 7:00 a.m. tomorrow morning," she said before leaving.

After the woman had left Dee said, "I want to rest until the event starts in the morning."

"That's a very good idea!" Solomon said in agreement.

Once she was settled in bed, he went to tuck her in and drew lines in the palms of her hands as he always did. Dee slept through the night and woke up early in the morning feeling refreshed. She scurried to her dad's room and found him still sleeping. Next, she went to Uncle U's room, but he wasn't there. She found him sitting on a chair facing the door. He was always hyper-vigilant when it came to their personal security.

Dee sensed her dad moving about and hurried back to his room. Solomon stretched, yawned and rubbed his eyes. He reached for his old pocket watch, and after noting the time he said, "You are up early this morning, Little D. Let's order some breakfast." They ordered a bowl of fresh fruits and some raw broccoli for Dee, and the men ate an assortment of fruits and some pancakes.

There was a knock at the door shortly after they finished eating. U answered, and it was the woman in red from yesterday. However, this time she was wearing all orange—from her orange hair down to her orange shoes. Dee jokingly remarked, "She shouldn't wear orange because it doesn't go well with her light blue color" (aura). The woman overheard her, and said with a chuckle, "If I had known that earlier, I would have worn a different color, but there's no time for me to change now. I'm here to dress the child for the event."

"I can dress myself!" Dee quickly announced.

So the lady excused herself and left. Dee went into her room to put on the silver jumpsuit, shoes and socks. Then she went to show her dad. Solomon adjusted her clothing and tied the silver cloth around her head according to her directions. It was to be wrapped three times and then tied in a knot.

They were ready to go and headed out the door when Solomon remembered that Dee would need the crystal key. U retrieved it from the bag and gave it to him. They left the room and were headed the wrong way. They were redirected by a man dressed in all white that seemed to be waiting for them. He led them to the lower level, then down an all-white hallway with a green line on the floor to the right and a yellow line to the left. They continued until they reached a red door. U stepped through first and was greeted by the sound of loud cheering which soon stopped when the crowd realized he was not a participant. Solomon handed Dee the crystal key and said, "I will be right behind you when you walk through that door, so stay focused on your task."

As Dee stepped through the door, the sun reflected off her silver suit. All the spectators rose to their feet enthusiastically, cheering and clapping for her. In front of her was the labyrinth, an enormous stone edifice in the middle of the Coliseum. Six other participants stood in front of their respective pedestals near each of the seven separate entrances. Dee was number seven and walked over to the vacant pedestal. She noticed that everyone had inserted their crystal keys into the key slot on their pedestals, so she did the same. Dee turned to face the audience, and the clapping and cheering began to subside. Solomon and U stood on either side of her.

The escort who had met them was on a balcony above the participants. He was wearing an all pink suit, and spoke to the audience and then to each participant. In turn, each participant addressed the audience in the native language of their respective country. Dee had the ability to comprehend the gist of many different languages, and she understood that they were thanking their countries and certain people who had helped them. When the time came for Dee to speak, Solomon stepped forward on her behalf. Unfortunately, unlike the other participants, Dee's wasn't honored by her county, so her dad didn't have much to say.

After all the participants had made their statements, the official began to call each one of the seven colors they wore, and each participant stepped forward with their hand raised. The first participant was a fair-skinned man in purple; the second, who was in his 40s and also had the distinction of being the oldest man, wore blue; and the third man was in green. The fourth was an Asian male in his 20s; the fifth was an older Indian man in his 30s, wearing orange. The sixth was a man in red, and the seventh was Dee, the only child, and female in the event.

The official in the pink suit instructed the participants to watch the red lights at the openings of their labyrinths, and when the light turned green, they were to enter. Then a man in a brown business suit walked out of the red doors and approached the first participant at the first pedestal. He spoke to each participant separately and gave them final directions to make sure they were clear about their goals.

Dee was the final participant he talked to, and he explained the goals to her as simply as he could, while Solomon listened in. She was to find the center of the labyrinth where she would see a crystal bowl resting on a pedestal. The bowl was extensively fractured and very fragile and must be handled with extreme caution. She was to retrieve the crystal bowl and place it on her pedestal outside the labyrinth while it still was still intact. He warned her that if the sun's rays were to touch the crystal bowl, it most likely would shatter in her hands, and she would not complete the event.

Dee didn't really understand everything the man explained, but she understood the purpose of the task was to find the crystal bowl in the center and place it on the pedestal outside without breaking it. She also was told that a prize would be awarded if she completed the task, in addition to the invitations she would receive to the mystery schools. Her dad had gone to great lengths to gain her admission into the special schools, and completing the task was important to accomplish that goal so Dee would try her best. Solomon made sure Dee understood what to do, and she assured him that she did.

Once each participant had received their individual instructions, the man in the brown suit sent a signal to the official up above. The walls of the labyrinth opened up, exposing the seven entrances. The lights to each entrance changed from red to green, and all the participants rushed inside, all except Dee. She stood still for a few moments in no rush; she didn't want to enter at the same time as the others.

The audience began to murmur as Dee remained near the pedestal. The official asked Solomon if she was all right, and Solomon raised his hand to say all was okay. Dee looked towards her dad and turned in a full circle to place an energy shield around her body. She slowly walked into the labyrinth and her second sight clicked on automatically. She made a right turn and looked back, and could no longer see her father.

Dee continued walking for a quite a while and made several turns. She paused to look up at the sky and realized that the spectators were able to track the participants' progress through the labyrinth by the reflections their suits made when the sun shone on them. The different colored uniforms looked like small lights navigating through the pathways of the giant labyrinth. She began to skip along and explore where all the turns led. She could see low energy beings, sliding doors that opened into darkness, and vicious looking sun-shaped faces.

A horrible noise emanated from the darkness at one turn, and she investigated by bravely sticking her head right into it. There was nothing more than the energy of the sound. She continued exploring the labyrinth, skipping along, until she realized that she had been inside for a long time and was not focusing on her task, as her father had asked her to do. Dee got back on track, determined to complete the challenge.

Then she heard the audience yelling and cheering again. Using her abilities to see beyond the walls of the labyrinth, Dee saw the participant wearing blue in her mind's eye. He had exited the labyrinth with his crystal bowl still intact and cloaked from the sun by his shadow. As he attempted to place the crystal bowl on his pedestal, the rays of the sun touched the bowl, and it shattered in his hands. He fell to his knees distraught and remained on the ground.

Using her abilities, Dee was able to check the progress of the other participants. She was surprised to find the red contestant sitting with his knees drawn up to his chest, and his eyes shut tight as if he was frightened. She scanned for the other participants. They all seemed to be in similar circumstances. They were lost, confused or desperately trying to exit the labyrinth without securing their crystal bowls.

Dee continued walking while staying focused on the task. Then she saw a flicker of light coming from the corner to her right. She walked towards it and turned the corner to find the room flooded with light coming from her crystal bowl. It was on a tall pedestal in a shaded area and out of her reach because she was so small. Dee had to find a way to get the bowl without breaking it. After thinking about it for a moment, she used her magick and drew an energy circle around the base of the pedestal. She then made the pedestal descend into the ground enough for her to reach her hand into the bowl.

Dee began rubbing her hands together, making them glow with blue energy. She placed her right hand inside the bowl while releasing some of the energy from her hand into it. Dee began stirring the released energy inside the bowl like her mom would mix cake batter. This protected the crystal bowl from breaking. Then she blew on her hands once to stop the energy. Then picked up the bowl and began finding her way out of the labyrinth.

After some time and much focus, Dee made her last turn. She saw her father standing near the pedestal. When he saw her, he smiled and took four steps backward. The spectators stood up and gasped as one. They were apparently shocked to see the little girl exiting the sacred labyrinth with her crystal bowl fully intact in her hands, and completely unaffected by the sun's rays.

When Dee exited the labyrinth, she felt a power surging through her mind and body that she had never felt before. She took the final steps to her pedestal and held the bowl directly up to the sun. The combination of the sunlight through the crystal bowl, along with her energy and the reflection from her silver jumpsuit filled the arena with millions of tiny bright lights floating through the air. There was so much bright light that the spectators had to shield their eyes, causing their view of Dee to be distorted. The girl took four more steps towards the pedestal. She used her magick to reach high enough to place the crystal bowl on its resting place. The man in the white suit that was near Dee's pedestal immediately covered the crystal bowl with a cloth. He bowed to her and made his way back to near the exit door. The spectators cheered wildly, and her dad picked her up. "I love you, Little D! You did it!" he said with pride and excitement in his voice. She looked over a U and saw him raise his hands in victory.

The spectators were still cheering when the official in the pink suit approached the microphone. When the cheers finally died down, he announced,

"This is a day to be remembered. This is to be recorded so that all will know. Throughout the history of this event, no one has ever completed this task before!"

The spectators began to cheer wildly again. Dee felt that her powerful magick was at her command. At that moment, she knew that she could use the power of her mind to instantly manifest her desires. Nonetheless, true to her loving heart and supreme humility, she only wanted to use that moment to help the other participants who were desperately trying to exit the labyrinth. Solomon put her down and stepped away, looking very proud of his young daughter.

"Spoon boy: Do not try and bend the spoon. That's impossible. Instead... only try to realize the truth. That there is no spoon then you'll see that it is not the spoon that bends, it is only yourself."

The Matrix (1999)

Dee knew she would have to make a pathway to free the other participants. She walked to the labyrinth and placed her hands on the walls. Using the power of her mind in conformity with her will, the seven labyrinth entrances became long straight pathways that lined up so that each contestant could easily exit. The audience was stunned into silence as Dee displayed her powerful magick right in front of them. All the participants walked out looking disheveled but relieved. They were astonished at her display of power. They formed a single line, and the blue participant joined them, and everyone bowed to her one at a time and went back to their pedestals.

The man in the white suit opened the exit door and directed the trio to go through now that the event was over. They began making their way back to the room, and Dee said, "Hey, there's a rainbow behind the door." U walked back to the door to open it and saw the man in white standing with the other participants in all the different colored jumpsuits. "There's your rainbow, Little D," said Solomon. Dee laughed at what she saw. They continued up the steps and Dee could sense that many people were waiting to see her. "How were they able to get there so quickly?" Solomon wondered out loud.

He placed her on his shoulders, making it harder for anyone to touch her. They walked through the next door, where U was already waiting.

"That was extraordinary, Little D! You're the one. Just wonderful," said U as he patted her on the back and opened the door for them. They passed through to the hallway on the other side, where the official dressed in pink waited to write notes in Solomon's journal. He hastily scribbled something on the pages and slammed it shut. Turning to Dee and Solomon, he began excitedly talking about the historical event that everyone had just witnessed.

Wanting to get to their room so that they could sleep, Solomon interrupted him. "We're tired and need to rest." The man asked if he could walk with them to their room and Solomon agreed. He continued trying to speak with Solomon as they walked, but her dad was preoccupied with Dee's protection. Many of the spectators were now in the halls, waiting to see her, and even though Solomon had her hoisted up on his shoulders, some of them were trying to reach towards the special child to touch her. U tried to block them with his large frame, but there were just too many of them. Dee could feel their negative energies every time they placed their hand on her foot. She knew that she was not supposed to be touched at that point, and especially by them. So she used her powerful magick and created an energy shield around the group.

They now moved smoothly through the crowd because everyone that came in contact with Dee's energy field froze in place. Only after the group passed were the people able to move again. The man in pink was also within Dee's protective shield, but he was so preoccupied trying to get Solomon's attention that he didn't even notice her magick. The intrusive crowd seemed confused as to what was happening to them once they were released from their temporary frozen state.

When the trio finally reached their room, the man in pink whispered something to Solomon and then took his leave. At last, they were behind the locked doors of their room and could get some rest. They slept through the night and left very early the next morning. Dee was still tired when they woke her to leave, and she slept for most of the flight back home.

Solomon said ruefully to U, "If Dee had been born in Asia, India or one of the other countries that were represented by the participants; she would be honored and given the keys to the country." U agreed. "It's a real shame; those people are not worthy to be in your presence or witness your child's gifts."

Once they arrived home, Dee never told anyone of the feats she had accomplished and nobody ever asked where she went or what she did when she traveled with Solomon. She returned home to be teased and ridiculed by her clueless half-siblings as usual.

The Opera and the Cave Ritual

Dee, Solomon, and U were off to France to have documents signed so Dee could attend the mystery schools. Customarily, escorts or translators would meet them at their destination, but this time was different. They caught a cab and went to the hotel on their own accord. Once they had checked in, Solomon made some calls, and a short time later they were on their way.

After a short cab ride, they arrived at their contact's location. The building looked like a deserted museum. True to form, inside was an extensive collection of nude sculptures of various shapes and sizes. Some of them were half human-half animal, while others were of humans or animals. While Solomon was engaged in conversation with his contact, U and Dee walked around to take a closer look at the displays.

What was interesting was that the statues at the front of the exhibit were all white figures. As U and Dee progressed through the room, the statues displayed were all brown colored. When they reached the furthest point in the back, all the statues were black and much older looking. The placement was not lost on U, and he mentioned it to Dee while they were walking back to Solomon. They saw him still engaged inconversation with his contact.

Solomon was told that they would need to attend an opera that evening to rendezvous with the man whose signature was required on documents needed for Dee's admittance into the mystery schools. "All the arrangements have been made," Solomon advised U. "We just need to give our names to the usher upon arrival at the Opera House, and then we can sit and enjoy the performance. Afterward, the man will find us and sign the documents." He continued, "I was told that we will most likely be invited to his home and that we should accept the invitation."

The group had time to kill before attending the opera that evening. So they decided to go sightseeing and souvenir shopping. They stopped to dine alfresco at one of the many sidewalk cafes the city had to offer. Their exploration was over a few hours later, and they returned to their hotel room with plenty of time to freshen up and change into appropriate attire for the evening's agenda.

On arrival at the Opera House, an usher approached Solomon. Once he had identified himself, they were escorted to exclusive box seats in the balcony. Dee was too short to sit in the seats and see the stage, so they accommodated her with an overstuffed pillow on her seat. This worked perfectly, and she was able to gaze at the audience below and marvel at how they were dressed. It was bizarre because they were all in costume and had masks covering their faces. No other children were in attendance, and the trio were the only attendees not in costume. U noticed that the only other person of color in the audience was a black man seated next to a white woman. He pointed it out to Solomon and jokingly said, "We're not the only black people in the place for once."

The audience went silent as the performance began. There was not even a polite applause at the first notes of the overture. The odd behavior continued throughout the performance, and even at the end, no one applauded. The performance depicted an event that had occurred in a small French town, but Dee wasn't clear on exactly what the event was or where it took place because she was just a child.

After the performance ended, the audience remained seated and silent. Once the rest of the cast had cleared the stage, two men dressed in white costumes bearing swords appeared. They began to duel, and Dee quickly realized that the display wasn't acting. Their clothing wasn't even made of the standard Kevlar material typically used to protect fencers. The men were literally cutting each other with their foils. It was a macabre scene as blood saturated the white of their costumes.

In the end, both men fell to the ground bloodied, and emergency medical personnel entered the stage to care for them. The audience still did not applaud, but they turned their attention to the balconies above and behind them. Dee thought for a moment that everyone was looking at her group but quickly realized their attention was directed towards the neighboring box where a man and woman sat. The man wore a mask with four horns on the head, one on either side and one in the front and back. He made a gesture, and the audience began exiting the theatre as silently as they had been throughout the performance.

The woman from the next box came over to Dee's group and greeted Solomon, and U. Then she asked Dee if she had enjoyed the opera. "No!" Dee answered honestly and abruptly. "The men were hurting each other." The woman gazed at her strangely, nodded and then walked away without saying another word. Then the masked man with the horns entered. He took off his disguise and greeted Solomon. Getting right down to business, he asked for the documents that required his signature. Solomon produced them, along with his journal. The man wrote in the journal and signed the papers on the spot. He told Solomon that arrangements had been made for them to go to Russia. Once there, a helicopter would take them to another event where they would meet the directors in charge of one of the mystery schools. He would arrange to have an interpreter accompany them on the journey. The man then extended an invitation for the group to come to his home, stating that he had something to give to Solomon.

The invitation was graciously accepted without hesitation, and they all left the theatre together. A driver was provided that took the trio to the man's home. The drive took an hour, as most of the roads leading there were steep and winding. When they pulled up outside, they were in awe of the size and beauty of the mansion. It looked more like an exclusive fancy hotel than a private home.

They were greeted at the door by their host, who had a short conversation with Solomon, before indicating that they should continue the conversation in his office. Dee and U were left to their own devices in the reception area. They looked around admiring the large artworks on the walls. Soon, a butler wearing a black and white uniform appeared and offered them a tour of the home. U accepted the offer.

The home was impressive, boasting large rooms and a two-story library. There were rare edition books kept on the second level which required the presence of the master himself for access. In one of the rooms was the largest table Dee had ever seen. She told U that the man must have a lot of children to have such a large table. The guide and U both chuckled at her innocent comment. The guide explained to her that the room was reserved for special functions. U quickly lost his smile and returned to his usual serious demeanor.

The next room was luxuriously appointed with reclining chairs, tables, couches and dim lamps. It was clear that this was the smoking room because of the lingering odor of cigarettes, and also the scattered boxes filled with the finest cigars. The tour was cut short by the sound of a soft bell, apparently beckoning their guide. Dee and U were escorted back to the reception area, where Solomon was waiting for them. He was carrying a small briefcase that he didn't have when they arrived. Their host was thrilled that they'd been given a tour of his home. He asked if they had been shown the indoor swimming pool, and boasted that it was the most impressive room in the whole house, complete with a massive waterfall. He invited the group to be his guests anytime, and he would provide all the arrangements. He went on to say, "I know you don't have time to stay now, as you have to be in Russia tomorrow, but please come back soon." Solomon thanked their host, and they returned to the hotel to pack up their belongings. Then Solomon made some calls before they left for Russia.

The chartered flight from Paris to Koltsovo, Russia took several hours and was uneventful. Dee slept through most of the flight, as she usually did, and Solomon and U took turns keeping an eye on her while the other was napping. Once in Russia, the journey continued by helicopter as promised, taking them somewhere in the Ural Mountains, where they landed on a remote mountaintop. It was freezing on the mountain, and they fought the wind as they made their way to the entrance. It was a massive castle built into the side of the mountain, very isolated and hard to see unless you were as close to it as they were. It was enormous and had gargoyle sentries carved from rock far above.

A short flight of stairs carved from the rock of the mountain took them to the large entrance door. Inside the anteroom, the walls were smooth and quite cool. They were escorted by the interpreter and a woman to a large room with high ceilings. There was a large triangle design above, and the only furniture in the room was a long wooden table with six chairs on either side. A large custom-made chair designed for two occupants sat at the head. It was somewhat reminiscent of the chair that Dee and Solomon had shared when she had witnessed her first self-sacrifice ritual sometime before.

However, that one had a gargoyle carved into the backrest. The woman advised them through the interpreter that dinner would be served there once all the guests were present. In the meantime, she would show them to their room and would collect them when it was time to gather in the dining area.

On the way to their room, U marveled at the construction of the mountain hideaway. Their escort explained that much work had gone into modernizing it for more comfort. The hallways had been widened as well as the surrounding rooms so that they wouldn't lose any square feet. Once they settled into their room, they saw that the bathroom was no less a marvel. It featured a large pond continuously being fed water by a source from within the wall. Candles were distributed on a ledge carved from the rock, and a small table in an hourglass shape stood in the middle of the pond.

Dee was anxious to get into the water and Solomon cautioned her to be careful because the bottom looked slippery. She dipped a foot in first, and once she was sure she wouldn't slip, the rest of her body followed. Dee immediately felt refreshed, and her skin felt as though it was tingling. *This is obviously not the same type of water that regular people drank or bathe in,* she thought. It seemed that with every mouthful of water Dee drank, her body felt more hydrated than ever. The constant flow of water made her feel like she was in a stream. She spent quite a bit of time in the water before getting out and toweling herself dry with the luxurious towels that had been provided.

Dee got dressed and returned to the main room. She noticed that the furnishings were made of stone and were all adorned with pillows and throws. There were paintings, murals, and carvings on all the walls. Dee expressed her wonder at how spectacular the place was, and Solomon and U were equally impressed. Then a distant echo of a knock resounded through the room. The woman had returned to escort them to dinner.

They followed her to the dining area and saw that the guests were already standing behind their seats. The chair at the head of the table remained vacant, as well as the one to its immediate right, which was reserved for U. A man stood next to U with a strange grin on his face as he looked at Dee. She not only noticed the man's odd behavior but also noticed he was making U very uncomfortable and tense. U held the man's gaze, and his expression quickly changed, and he scurried away.

A signal was given directing Dee and Solomon to be seated at the head of the table. Once they sat down, the remaining guests took their seats. U sat next to Solomon and servers entered the room holding platters covered with shiny silver domes, and placed one in front of each guest. A bell rang, and the guests removed the covers from their plates. A sommelier made his way around the table and poured red wine into the silver goblets in front of each guest. He was about to pour some for Dee, but Solomon placed his hand over the goblet, indicating that they would pass on the wine.

Solomon engaged in conversation with the man and woman seated next to him, as well as with Dee. They were directors of one of the mystery schools, and they both assured him that his daughter would be safe and well protected, and would be a great addition to the school when it was her time to attend. "And just like the other pupils, she would be both student and teacher," said the lady director while winking at Dee. Since Dee didn't understand the gesture, she politely asked the director not to do that. The woman nodded at Dee as her dad and U looked on.

When dinner was over, the guests began preparing for the next part of the evening. Three steps up from the dining area was a circular room with railing carved from stone surrounding it. It overlooked a pit of sorts. In the pit was a white woman dressed in white clothing with black circle designs on the fabric. It was a strange room filled with sharp weapons ranging from knives to swords of all sizes. It wasn't so much the weapons themselves that made the room strange; it was that they were all blade-up, with their hilts firmly embedded into the rock walls. One sword in the middle of the room had its hilt deeply embedded in the ground like Excalibur, only reversed.

Music began playing, echoing off the stone walls. The woman in the pit began to dance around the blades. As she swayed, her body passed one of the swords, and the blade cut her. The onlookers in the Vista above gasped. The woman continued to dance in spite of the bleeding, pirouetting into another blade protruding from the wall and impaling herself on her right side. She slowly disengaged from the blade and applied pressure to the bleeding wound. There was a large volume of blood coming from the injury, and it was clear that the blade had done severe damage. She fell to the floor, and everyone thought she had completed the ritual—but that wasn't the case. She stood once more and moved awkwardly towards the sword situated in the middle of the room, and fell onto it. The sword pierced through her body, and the woman lay dead. The dance was over.

The leader of the group turned to Solomon and asked, "Do you understand what you have just witnessed?" Solomon did not answer. "That woman had not fulfilled her duty, which was an egregious transgression that brought shame to both our members and her family," he said. "In order for her to preserve the dignity and honor of her family, the ritual was voluntarily performed."

"Was her family notified of her decision to perform the ritual?" Solomon asked.

The man pointed out a gentleman in a black suit standing at the rail wiping tears from his eyes. "That is her brother," said the leader.

The guests began leaving the cave, but the trio remained behind, as they were not scheduled to depart until the next morning.

Once back in their room, Dee sat with her dad on the balcony staring up at the starry night. It was a beautiful clear night, so clear that the gargoyle sentries atop the castle seemed alive and ready to take flight. U took some time to enjoy the pond and eventually joined them on the balcony. "That was the most refreshing bath I have ever taken in my life," said U. "It must be the underground fresh water or something. I will never forget this trip, but the people are very peculiar." They discussed the events of the evening and U expressed his unhappiness with the man who had stared at Dee. "I thought he was surely a pedophile. I also don't understand why such a high price had to be paid by the woman," he said. "She had sworn an oath and broken it, and the ritual was the only way, in their view, to rectify that broken vow," said Solomon.

The next day during the flight home, Dee heard her dad complaining about taking his daughter so far to see yet another ritual sacrifice. "We did what needed to be done, and I'm glad it's over," he said. "She can begin attending the mystery schools when she turns twelve." He began writing in his journal, which he always carried with him, as Dee drifted off to sleep.

The Travel Agent

One evening Solomon informed Dee that they were going to visit an old friend of his who lived so far away that it would take two more days to get to his home even after the plane landed in his country. But before they left, Solomon needed to visit the Shaman to get something to help him tolerate the long journey. He would only be gone for a few hours and when he returned he wanted Dee to be ready to go. He called for her mom. "Ella, feed Dee and wash and braid her hair while I'm gone. I'll be back soon."

Ella prepared a cooked meal for her children and gave Dee her customary raw fruits and vegetables. Everyone sat quietly as they ate, and once done, her mom began packing their bags. Then Ella refolded her clothes in the drawers and plaited Dee's and Emma's hair. Afterwards, Emma asked Dee to go outside with her to play. Emma had never invited Dee to play with her before. Emma knew that Solomon had told Dee to stay inside. "I might not see you for a very long time, so we should play before you leave," said Emma.

Dee declined, "Dad told me to stay inside until he comes back." Emma responded by sticking her tongue out and calling her a "Daddy's girl," as she headed out the door to play with her brother Fred. Dee wasn't bothered at all by what Emma had done, and she liked being called a "Daddy's girl." What Emma intended as an insult actually made Dee feel good.

Dee entertained herself by drawing until her father returned with U in tow. She hadn't seen U in a while. Dee jumped down from her dad's special chair and ran over to him. "Hello, Uncle U!" Dee said as she punched him in the leg. He would always feign injury when she did that.

"Just a little harder and you would be quite the puncher," said U.

"I could never hurt you, Uncle U," she said, as he picked her up.

"We protect each other, right, Dee?" U asked.

"That's right!" Dee replied.

Solomon came out of his room and announced that they were running late and needed to leave right away. He asked U to grab the luggage which included a big footlocker that he needed to bring along.

U picked up the luggage and loaded the car while Solomon went inside to find Ella. He came outside with Ella at his side just as Uncle U was giving Dee a shoulder ride around the car. U seemed happier than usual about going on this trip for some reason. Solomon kissed Ella goodbye and gave her some money for anything that she might need while he was away. U handed Dee to her mom, who hugged her tightly and whispered, "Be good for your dad and Uncle U, and do not hurt anyone." Dee replied, "Don't worry, Mom, I'm always good."

They drove away and headed to the airport where Solomon met a nervous looking white man wearing glasses and a dark gray suit. Dee and U stayed back as Solomon spoke with him, but when the man reached into his suit pocket, U moved closer to Solomon. U watched as the man's hand slipped from view, and because he was already wary of the stranger, he stepped even closer to Solomon. The man retracted his hand and gave Solomon an envelope and U's shoulders relaxed slightly, but he kept on slowly walking towards them. The man then reached into his pants pocket and retrieved a small black pouch. By this time U was standing right next to Solomon, seemingly still concerned for his safety. Dee, on the other hand, was not concerned about the man at all. She could read his energy and knew he wasn't a threat. In fact, he was as nervous as he appeared to be.

The man looked skittishly around before stammering to Solomon that he didn't feel safe conducting such business at the airport. Solomon assured him that they were safe and advised him to bring some security men along next time so he would feel more secure. The man nodded, shook Solomon's hand and looked around once more before quickly walking away.

The airport was crowded, and people were waiting in long lines. The trio bypassed the lines and headed directly to customs at a fast pace. Dee asked her dad why they were walking so quickly. "We need to move quickly because those who watch us would rather we were poor and stayed in one place so that they can keep better track of us," he told her. "This trip is for our business and enjoyment."

Their travel agent was waiting outside the customs office for them. She was a white woman with long black hair and had been Solomon's travel agent for many years. She always made sure he had a well-planned itinerary when he traveled. She warmly greeted them all and then kneeled to reach out for Dee, who stepped back and hid behind her dad's leg, as she usually did when the travel agent tried to touch her.

"Did you have any problems making any of the arrangements?" Solomon asked.

"Not at all, everything is in order," she replied. They all walked to the gate where a private plane was standing by.

Before going out the gate and boarding, Solomon thanked the travel agent for her many years of service and said, "I have a gift for you, and you may not want to work for me anymore once you receive it." The travel agent seemed surprised and said, "I love working for you, Mr. Solomon, and you pay me well enough already, so gifts are not necessary." Solomon smiled as he handed her the black pouch and envelope he had received from the nervous looking man a short time ago.

She opened the pouch and pulled out a beautiful large diamond. She looked stunned and her eyes filled with tears. She then opened the envelope and read what was inside as she wiped the tears from her eyes. When she had finished reading, the woman fell to her knees kissing Solomon's shoes. U stepped forward and gently helped the woman back to her feet because people were staring at them.

"There is no need for such effusive behavior," said Solomon. "I have given you the gift to thank you for the many years of excellent care and service you have provided."

The travel agent interjected and said, "I was just doing my job that you pay me very well to do. But what you have given me will take care of my family and me for the rest of our lives."

In her happiness, the woman hugged U, who quickly extricated himself. He reminded her that people were always watching them. She looked around and nodded in agreement saying, "Of course, you're right." She then bent down to Dee and said, "You and your father are very special and important." She had a big smile on her face as she reached her hand out to touch Dee. This time, instead of stepping away, Dee allowed the travel agent to gently touch her face for the first time.

The woman kept her gaze fixed on Dee until Solomon placed his hand on his daughter's shoulder and said, "It's time to go." The travel agent escorted them to the plane. Once seated, Dee looked out of the window and saw her standing by the terminal door. Dee could see with her second sight that the travel agent had an energy glow that would last her a long time, and her dad was responsible for it. The plane started to taxi down the runway and in no time they were off.

The full memory of this trip has never been fully recovered. However, Dee remembers being on an island and spending a lot of time with a brown-skinned native lady who taught her different things about nature, the ocean and the sky. Dee also spent time with another teacher who taught proper etiquette. When her dad left her alone with that lady, she would immediately correct Dee's posture and hold her chin up high with a small stick. As Dee was being taught by the women, Solomon and U tended to other business on their own, the nature of which Dee was unaware.

Egypt: The Funeral and the Pyramid Ritual

One evening, Dee sat with her mom on the couch in the living room. The half-siblings were all outside playing and not including her as usual. Using her senses, Dee was able to predict when the phone would ring. So when she felt the phone's energy in the air, she would immediately tell her mom that it would soon ring. So, Dee advised her mom about a call that was coming through, and sure enough a short time later, the phone rang. Ella jumped as if she was startled, and got angry at Dee, even though she was just trying to help her mom. "How many times do I have to tell you, never say when the phone is going to ring?" Ella demanded. "Just wait until it actually rings!"

Ella answered, and the caller asked for Solomon. He took the phone from his wife and seemed surprised that the caller was able to locate him, and said, "We may not make it in time, but we will be there." After hanging up, he stood thinking for a moment. "Who was it?" Ella asked. Solomon was still with his thoughts and did not reply. Ella seemed curious. "The operator told me it was an international call," she said.

"It was a call from a place outside of Cairo," Solomon replied.

"Where is Cairo?" Ella asked.

"I know, I know! I want to answer," said Dee.

Her mom hushed Dee because she wanted Solomon to answer. "Let Dee answer; she may know," her dad said. Ella was not happy with this. After all, Dee was just a child and surely wouldn't know because she hadn't attended any school. Solomon ignored Ella's complaints and waited for Dee's answer.

"Cairo is in Egypt!" Dee shouted.

"That's correct, Little D. Great!" Solomon said with a smile.

Ella had a surprised look on her face. "How did she know that?"

"It doesn't matter," Solomon replied. "We will have to leave this evening and will be gone for at least a week. A relative on my mother's side of the family just died, and I am expected to attend the ceremony."

Solomon stepped out of the room and Ella took the opportunity to call Dee a "smart ass" before she left and went outside. Dee didn't understand her mom's angry reaction to her. Her son Alex always got good grades in school, and her mom gushed over him and bragged about how impressed she was with his intellect. Dee couldn't understand why her mom was so different with her. She quickly forgot about it because she was happy to be leaving with her dad soon.

Before they left that evening, Solomon gave Ella some envelopes that needed to be delivered to a location not far from town the following morning. Ella was still upset with Dee and was not pleased with having been tasked with the errands. "Why can't one of the boys deliver the envelopes for you?" Ella asked as if she was annoyed. "The last time I tasked your son Wilson with this, he stopped to visit his girlfriend first, and the men waiting for the delivery were agitated," advised Solomon. "He arrived late and unapologetically admitted that he made a stop to see a girlfriend. These were serious men that wanted to teach him a 'man's lesson,' but because of Wilson's connection to me, they didn't." Ella finally acquiesced, and Solomon further instructed her not to say a word to anyone when she dropped off the envelopes. "I already gave the boys some money, so do not give them anymore," he said. He knew they were notorious for tricking their mother out of her money.

Solomon and Dee left for Cairo that night. Uncle U didn't accompany them on this trip, and Dee remembers sleeping a lot during the flight. They arrived at their destination and remained on the plane until the two other passengers on board had disembarked. Then a man boarded the plane and greeted her dad. He had clothes for Dee to wear and advised that she change into them before they deplane. Solomon helped her dress in the local garb which included a veil that covered her face. Dee felt important wearing the clothing. After dressing, she sat quietly in her seat looking out the window and could see men loading their bags into one of the two cars on the tarmac.

They were escorted to the car, and Dee glanced at the terminal and could see people watching them from the windows. As they drove through the city, children ran up to the car to wave, and Dee waved back to them. They drove through the desert until the car stopped near a group of men who were waiting by some camels. Some of the men greeted them, but Dee's attention went straight to the camels. It was the first time she had ever seen a camel, and she was delighted. She could see the energy of fat in their humps, and Solomon explained that the camels were able to travel a long way in the desert without the need for water. The men informed Solomon that they would have to travel the rest of the way by camel.

The camel that Dee and Solomon were to ride had a tiny shelter on the back hump. When the camel was brought forward, the man had the animal bend down so that she and Solomon could get on. With her dad's permission, he lifted Dee into the little shelter and then assisted Solomon into the saddle. Dee wanted to sit with her dad, but he told her he would have to learn how to manage the camel first. They began the first part of their journey with a man walking alongside them instructing Solomon on how to maneuver the camel. It was not long before he felt confident enough to manage on his own. The man who would lead the caravan mounted his camel and went to the head of the line. He waved his hand, and the caravan started moving at a faster clip.

Solomon called Dee to come forward now, but there was nothing for her to see except dunes made of pink and white sand. So Solomon instructed her to go back inside and take a nap, promising that he would wake her up when they were close to their destination. Good to his word, Solomon woke her when they were nearing the end of the journey. Dee climbed back up front with him, wiping the sleep from her eyes. They were traveling through a path lined with date palms on either side. She looked to the rear marveling at the spectacle. Many camels had joined the caravan. Some were being ridden while others carried large bags on their backs while their owners walked beside them.

As the caravan approached the town, Dee saw women busy with many different occupations. Some were making bread, and others were cooking rice or grain. The children were busy putting fruits, nuts, and vegetables into large baskets. Young men carried jugs of water and wine, while young women carried long cloths across their arms. It looked as though they were all preparing for a great event.

They came to a stop near a stone wall that circled a substantial home. Their escort dismounted from his camel and called over to the guards at the gate. After a brief discussion, the guards walked to the camel that Dee and Solomon were on. The camel made a funny sound as it bent downward. This made Dee laugh as they were helped off.

They walked up the path to the great home, and a dark-skinned woman with very bright eyes hurried out to usher Dee inside. Solomon kissed Dee on the forehead before she left. She felt the woman's heartbeat as she hurried back inside carrying Dee in her arms. The woman took Dee to a room where there were many children and other women. Another woman approached Dee and introduced herself, as others gathered around. One of them told her not to be afraid, and although Dee wasn't afraid she said, "Okay." A woman removed Dee's veil and two women nearby covered their mouths and pointed to her hair.

The woman with the bright eyes spoke English and said they would bathe and fix her hair. She was happy about that after having been in the dust and heat of the desert for so long. When she asked for a drink of water one of the women rushed to bring her some, before taking her to a room to bathe. The room was cool, and Dee saw three other children bathing. She noted that one woman would bathe a child, a second woman would dry, and the third woman would take the children to another room containing many different clothes to dress them.

When Dee entered the large pool of water, a little girl getting washed next to her reached out her hand to touch Dee's hair. They began playing and continued until the woman took them out of the water. Once Dee was bathed, dried, dressed and fed, she was returned to her dad. "How was your bath, Little D?" Solomon asked. "It was great, but I can bathe myself without any help," she replied. Solomon smiled and explained that different cultures do things differently, and in Egypt, the children are pampered. Dee noticed the little girl she had bathed and played with waving at her across the room. So she asked her dad if it was okay to play with her new friend. Solomon seemed exhausted and said, "Sure, I need to rest anyway."

The girls ran hand in hand laughing as they went through the hallway. They came to a door and stopped to look inside. There was a group of men talking, and one of them spotted the girls and called for them to come in. The girl went to the man as Dee stayed put and looked in to see what was going on. The man was speaking quietly to the girl and looked over at Dee. The girl finished the conversation and rejoined Dee, and they continued running through the hallway. They eventually entered a room where other children were playing. Some were listening as older children read stories to the younger ones. Dee and her new friend walked through to an adjoining room that was empty. This is where they played. They began jumping up and down on the huge pillows scattered about the floor until they were finally exhausted. They rested for a while and rejuvenated, then they played hide and seek. They even indulged in a grand pillow fight. It seemed like they had been in the room for hours when the woman with the bright eyes came for them.

The two girls were escorted to a large room, where Dee saw her dad standing with a group of people. He was dressed in a long white tunic with white pants. She felt disheartened because the energy in the room was sad. She ran to her dad and held his hand, and a man approached and told him where to sit. She noticed that the area was separated by gender; men on one side, women on the other. The women were moving their tongues and making a wailing sound. The bright-eyed woman approached Solomon to escort Dee to the area where her new friend sat.

The ceremony began when an old man with a long white beard stood to speak, and all the wailing stopped. He was dressed like Solomon in a long white tunic and pants, but his tunic had long black and gold stripes in the front descending from the shoulders. A white turban was wrapped around his head and held together by a gold medallion decorated with jewels. The man proceeded to walk to a balcony decorated with different colored material draped over the edges. Most of the people outside stood up when the old man came to the balcony. When he began to speak, they all sat down to listen.

At the end of the ceremony, Solomon went to a room with the sons of the deceased royal lady. Dee and her new friend followed them and stood outside, one on either side of the doorway looking in on the men. They sat on rugs while talking and smoking hookahs. The old man that officiated the ceremony walked past the girls without saying a word and sat on a pillow next to the others. He spoke to one of the men, who then walked over to Solomon and instructed him to sit next to the old man. The old man didn't speak English, so he called one of the deceased lady's sons to be his interpreter. He spoke to Solomon through the interpreter, but the girls were too far away to hear.

The old man raised his hand, and another man got up and walked over to a wooden box draped with a silver and blue cloth. The cloth was removed, exposing a large wooden box decorated with carvings of horses. He opened the box and lifted a heavy looking medium sized gold chest and brought it to the old man. The old man opened the lid of the chest and motioned for Solomon, who then removed several pouches from inside.

Solomon opened each pouch and pulled out precious gems. He examined them one at a time, holding them to the light like an expert. Dee noticed that each stone he pulled out was different. There were diamonds, rubies, emeralds, sapphires, black diamonds, and others. Dee and her new friend looked on in amazement as Solomon examined each precious gem he pulled out. When he finished, he carefully placed each gem back into its respective pouches and back into the gold chest.

The process of doling out the inheritances continued, with one man receiving land and another receiving a small amount of white powder which he seemed very happy to get. However, Dee and her friend were not allowed to watch anymore. Bright Eyes had found them spying on the men and sent them to play in the children's room.

Solomon came to the children's room to retrieve Dee after the meeting ended, and the father of her new playmate accompanied him. They were discussing a visit to the pyramids the following day, and Dee had apparently been chosen out of all the children to take the special trip with the man's family.

Later that evening while Dee and her dad were in their room, she took some of the gems out of the pouches and played with them. They were all marble-sized and very shiny. Her dad saw her playing with them, but he did not seem to mind. "These will be yours someday, so be careful not to lose any of them," was his only comment. So, when she finished playing with the gems, Dee placed them back in the pouches all mixed up and went to bed.

That night Dee drifted off and began astral traveling. She traveled through the stars and glided along the rings of Saturn, a frequently visited destination. She plunged deep into the sun, before passing huge clusters of rocks resembling large planets. She woke to the feeling of warm air brushing her face, and opened her eyes and saw her playmate brushing a strand of hair away from her cheek.

Dee was in a car traveling through the desert, and her dad was sitting in the front seat along with her playmate's father who was driving. Two women and two children accompanied them including the girl she had played with and her little brother who sat in the back with Dee and the two women.

Solomon handed out snacks of figs and dates to the children once he saw them awake. The desert was hot, and Dee could see ripples of heat radiating from the sand as she drifted off to sleep again. She woke again to find the kids bouncing in the back seat. They had spotted some desert animals, probably a herd of gazelles, one of the few desert creatures in Egypt that were not nocturnal.

The driver became irritated with the commotion and requested that the women calm the children down. They sat quietly for a while, and soon they were all asleep again while holding hands. Dee was able to take them into her dreams. In this dreamland, there were many things to occupy them. They ran, played, yelled and laughed to their hearts' content in the surreal playground she had taken them to.

She awoke to one of the women arranging a black scarf about her face and head so that only her eyes could be seen. The same had been done to the other little girl. Solomon looked on and commented that all three children had laughed in unison while they slept. "It must have been a fun dream all of you had," he said.

At long last, they arrived at some pyramids. The sight took Dee completely by surprise. She felt an immediate connection to them and felt as if she wanted to fly around these geometric wonders. Seeing her attraction to the pyramids, her dad quietly told her to stay focused, as she was not alone and others may be watching her. He always seemed to know when his daughter entered a magical state, so she concentrated on the present.

Dee noticed many people dressed in the local attire. Some were sporting large colorful beads around their necks and walking with canes that had carvings of snakes and birds engraved into them. The old man that presided over the funeral was also on hand, along with the interpreter. He greeted Solomon and his party and touched the children on the head. Some other men and women standing by approached Solomon. One of the men asked, "Which one of these children was chosen?" The old man stepped forward with a hand on Solomon's and Dee's shoulder.

The man then turned to Solomon and directed him how to enter the pyramid. "You see the tall pillars; you are to walk past them, stop and look up at the statues before entering. Once inside, there will be a small glass pyramid where the chosen child must enter and be pulled up." Two bald men that would lead the group inside were carrying a small bench seat with no armrests or back and asked if they might have the honor of carrying the child on their chair. Solomon graciously declined and said that Dee would walk.

The procession into the pyramid was now being prepared. There was the question as to who would follow Dee into the pyramid. Solomon stated that he would be the one doing the honors. The two bald men would lead the way, and the others would follow.

That being settled, the group focused their attention on the attire Dee, and her dad would wear. Two women carrying boxes of clothing approached the group. A golden hat decorated with a triangle shape on the front and a round design on the back was placed on Solomon's head. He was then adorned with jewels placed around his neck, and finally, he was given a tall cane like the ones Dee had seen the others with.

Then it was Dee's turn. She was given a white dress that was placed over the black clothing she was wearing. The scarf which covered her face was removed, and jewels were placed around her neck. Dee's adornments included a beautiful gold piece that was put on her head. It had a golden eye carved in the front and was decorated with many small gems. Small rings were placed on her little fingers, and she was given two snake bracelets that wound up each arm. She was also presented with two small gold canes, one for each hand. As she was being dressed, Dee observed that the full red moon was making the night sky appear very bright and unusually red.

The woman tasked with dressing Dee stepped back to assess her work. Seeing that all was in place, she bowed and walked away. When Dee was fully adorned and ready to enter the pyramid, Solomon asked if she remembered what she had to do. She assured him that she did. "Take your time, Little D," he said. "I'll be right behind you, and if the weight of your adornments becomes too heavy, let me know." Dee stood still to check the weight, and they were indeed too heavy. She concentrated her energy on them, wanting to make them lighter. In an instant, they became light as a feather.

Dee maintained a comfortable distance from the two bald men leading the procession, as they had an energy that was not warm like the others. She stopped and paid tribute to the statues before entering the pyramid. Inside the musty smelling room were tall sculptures. Torches illuminated the room, and in the light, she could see hieroglyphics on the walls. She noticed a small glass pyramid with a small door on the front. She stood in front of the door with her dad at her side. The two bald men spoke a few words, and the remaining members of the party responded in unison.

Then the men turned and bowed to Dee before she entered. Her dad said, "It's like an elevator, Little D. They're going to take you up a bit and back down, so stay focused." On the other side of the room was a wheel with three long spindles. Two men began to turn the wheel, and the glass pyramid began to rise. Dee looked up as it made its ascent and she could see the light from the full red moon seeping through an opening at the top.

As she rose up, Dee's consciousness expanded and she became a red dot in the center of the blood moon. Keen to go on an out-of-body exploration, Dee had to stop herself and focus, as her dad had instructed her to do. She was able to exit that state, yet the light of the red moon was still emanating from her body. She yelled down to her dad, "Light will come from my body and spread across the room!"

"It's okay, Little D!" Solomon yelled back.

Suddenly a light beamed from her body so bright that the people below could no longer look up at her. She saw her dad spread his feet apart to maintain a stable stance as he held his canes in front of him. Those around him appeared mesmerized by the light, so she shielded her father and the men at the spindle from the light.

Soon, the light from Dee's body disappeared, and she saw everyone below her recover. The men lowered the glass pyramid, and she could still feel the energy of the red moon throughout her being. When she had descended all the way, Solomon opened the door and took her hand. The people in attendance made three circles around Dee and Solomon, the inner and outer circles moving clockwise, the middle circle moving counter-clockwise. The appearance of the counter rotating circles was almost hypnotic.

A short time later the people stopped moving, and Dee could hear them murmuring unfamiliar words. Then they made a path for her and her dad to exit the circles. Once outside the pyramid, the ceremonial jewels, canes and clothing that Dee and Solomon had been adorned with were removed and placed back in their boxes. With a final bow to Dee, the keepers of the adornments walked away.

The wind suddenly picked up as sand swirled around them, and everyone covered up and left. Dee fell asleep in Solomon's arms during the drive back. The next time she woke up, Solomon and the Shaman were at her side. The Shaman gave her an elixir of a brown powder and water he'd made.

"Where am I?" Dee asked.

"You're back in the US at the Shamans' home," Solomon said. "You've been asleep for several days, and I bought you here so that the Shaman could check on you when you awake."

Dee's only disappointment was that she hadn't said goodbye to her playmate.

A Royal Call

Dee and Solomon were enjoying some quiet time at home. He was reading a book in his special chair, and his daughter was coloring in her drawing book. She called out to her dad, "The phone is about to ring." He immediately got up to sit next to her, and no sooner had he sat down, the phone rang. He smiled at her as he picked up the receiver.

An acquaintance of his was on the other end. Solomon and the Shaman were requested to visit someone connected with the English royal family. One of the royals was in crisis, and it was thought that Solomon and the Shaman would be able to assist. They were asked to come as soon as possible, and arrangements had already been made to transport them.

When the call ended, Dee asked her father if she could go along. Dee hadn't been requested, and her dad didn't plan on taking her, so he asked, "Do you have a feeling about this trip, Little D?" Dee shook her head and said, "No, I just wanted to go with you." Her dad could not say no to her, so after calling U, they immediately began packing their bags, and soon left to see the Shaman.

Dee loved going to see the Shaman. It was a beautiful drive to his place, followed by a boat ride and concluding with a walk through the woods, as he lived deep in the bayou of Louisiana. When they arrived, they found the Shaman near the fire he always kept burning. While he and Solomon spoke, Dee entertained herself by investigating the wooden sculptures that the Shaman had carved, and all the plants he had growing in his gardens.

The Shaman agreed to accompany them, and they set off. Upon arrival at the airport, they had a short wait for U's flight to arrive. When U spotted them, they greeted each other warmly, and there were smiles all around. "Everything has been arranged for us," said Solomon. "They want us in the United Kingdom as soon as possible." The four of them boarded the empty plane and Dee fell asleep as soon as she settled into her seat.

When Dee woke up, she was in Solomon's arms. They had arrived in the UK and were walking with an escort to a vehicle. The escort opened the car doors for everyone to pile inside. Dee sat in the back seat with her dad and the Shaman, while U sat in the front with the driver. Dee noticed that the driver was on the right side of the car and found it funny. Solomon explained that the cars in that country are made that way.

Once in their hotel room, Solomon and the Shaman talked, while U thoroughly checked the room. Assured that everything was safe, Solomon put Dee to bed and tucked her in. "Have fun with the boy," her dad said before leaving.

The next morning, they all enjoyed breakfast, Dee eating her usual fresh fruits and vegetables. Then they headed out on foot to explore the city until it was time to leave. They visited several different shops as Solomon looked for souvenirs to bring home. He had long ago stopped asking Dee if there was anything she wanted because she was always very content. The only thing she really wanted, aside from visiting wild animals, was to attend the mystery schools to learn more about herself. To that end, they continued doing favors for influential people to ensure her successful admission.

The group returned to the hotel, and Solomon gave Dee a mineral tonic prepared by the Shaman. He instructed her to go wash up because they would be leaving soon. Not long after, there was a knock at the door, which U opened, to find a man wearing a coat that fell to his knees, along with a sash adorned with medals that ran across his chest. Greetings were exchanged, and the four travelers followed the man downstairs to a vehicle. Dee noticed that people were watching them as they walked through the lobby. So she asked her dad, "Why are the people staring?" Solomon explained, "The escort is a Royal Guard, and people don't often see them in person."

Dee sat on her dad's knee during the drive through the city so she could see the sights. First, they drove through the populated areas, and then made their way to the countryside, which seemed deserted by contrast. They arrived at a large stone wall that had a small guard house on either side. As they drove through the opening, a large home that resembled a castle came into view.

The Royal Guard led them through a large door adorned with a shield and a winged lion. Once inside, they saw people in the receiving room waiting to be summoned. They sat among them, though U remained standing behind Dee. Dee whispered, "The people look kind of strange. Why are they here?"

"They are here to try and help the lady, just as we are," her dad whispered back.

It was an eclectic group, including a monk, a cardinal, an Indian guru and an odd-looking man who wore garments similar to those of a witch doctor. They all were watching the Shaman and Dee.

Then the guard watching over everyone received a radio call. He approached Solomon to ask if they would prefer to walk in the gardens. A cardinal sitting nearby asked the guard why everyone wasn't permitted to walk in the gardens. The guard sternly replied, "These people were specifically invited."

Solomon thought a walk was a grand idea, so they followed the Royal Guard to a pathway into the lush grass. U told Solomon that the people in the room had been watching Dee squirm in her chair and it was a good idea for them to have left the area. They strolled through the gardens, marveling at the beauty. Tall hedges resembling a small labyrinth bordered each area. Dee began to focus on the hedges, and her dad noticed her interest. "No, Little D, we are not here for that," he said, chuckling. "I know, Dad!" said Dee.

They settled in a sitting area near the garden entrance to wait. Dee walked to a grassy patch to lie on her back and look up at the castle. She was distracted by a feeling that she was being watched. She looked up and to the right and saw a woman on a balcony looking down at her. U looked up to see what was holding Dee's attention and he too saw the woman. She waved to Dee, acknowledging her for the first time, and Dee waved back and got up to tell her father, "There's a lady on the balcony that has a lot of different energies in and around her head watching me," she said.

Solomon and the Shaman got up to look, but before they could make their way over, one of the guards beckoned them to follow him inside. They were led upstairs to a room with double doors. In that anteroom, they saw the guru they had seen earlier exiting an adjoining main room with red doors, escorted by a guard. Another guard came out of the room and asked Solomon if it would be all right if his daughter were to see the lady first. "The Shaman and I were requested, not my daughter," Solomon advised. The guard explained that the lady really wanted to see the child, and they understood that was not the original plan.

The Shaman pulled Solomon and Dee aside to speak in private. The Shaman asked Dee if she could help the lady with her sleeping problem.

"I'm not sure if she deserves my help," Dee replied. The Shaman smiled at her words and nodded to Solomon.

Solomon said, "If you help the lady, you may receive something that you will need in return."

Dee sighed heavily and reluctantly agreed to help. She marched to the red doors with the guard right behind her.

Inside the room was a lady lying on a bed designed like a sleigh with red coverings. Another woman was in the room standing by the bed. The woman had a big smile on her face as she said, "Look at the child. She is exactly as they told us she would be." The lady in the bed then told the guard and the woman to leave the room. They appeared very hesitant to leave her alone until she shouted at them, "Leave at once!" Startled by her outburst, they quickly left, and Dee was now alone with her.

The lady beckoned Dee to sit near her on the bed. It was too high for her to climb onto, so she directed her to the steps at the foot of the bed, and Dee climbed up easy`.

"Are you frightened of me?" the lady asked.

"No," Dee replied.

"Why are you here?" the lady asked.

"I wanted to travel with my father, and he allowed me to come along," Dee replied. "Why are you in bed?"

"Because I have been unable to sleep for days and it's causing my head to hurt." Then she frowned and said, "I refuse to take any of the drugs prescribed to me by the doctors."

Dee then asked, rather unexpectedly, "Why are you so mean to your helpers?"

The lady smiled. "The lack of sleep and my headache causes me to be short tempered and take my frustrations out on them."

"You shouldn't be mean to your helpers because one day you may need something from them," Dee advised.

"That's why I summoned people to help me sleep and relieve my headache so that I won't be mean," said the lady.

"The Shaman was the one who was called to help you, not me," said Dee.

The lady acknowledged this. "I only wanted to see you because I've been told that you could do for me what no others could do!" she cried out.

"If you want to sleep, you must first close your eyes and relax," Dee calmly told her.

When the lady closed her eyes, Dee was able to clearly see the energies in her head. She then instructed the lady to imagine her favorite thing to do while her eyes remained closed. The lady did as she was told and Dee felt her relax. Dee moved closer to her and placed her hands over the lady's eyes and evaluated the energy around her head. She saw that the energy for sleep was intertwined with that for thought. Dee corrected the energies, placing them back in their proper functions. She then closed her eyes and entered the lady's dream to verify that she was asleep. In the dream, she was on a large ship dancing with a tall man while looking up at him with a big smile on her face. Dee now knew the lady was sound asleep, so she left and closed the doors behind her. She immediately sat down on the floor by the doors.

Solomon, the Shaman, and U rushed up to Dee, as did the woman and the guard who had been in the room previously. Dee told them all that the lady was sleeping. The woman and the guard immediately entered the room to see for themselves. They came out a short time later, smiling, and confirmed that the lady was indeed sound asleep. "Well, since our task has been completed, we will be on our way," said Solomon. The guard pleaded with him to stay, as he was sure the lady would want to speak to them when she woke up. The woman offered them accommodations in a room she described as being quite lovely. Solomon declined. "I'd rather take my daughter to the hotel to rest after a long day, but thank you for the offer."

As they headed downstairs, Dee could hear a guard in the receiving area dismissing the remaining guests and advising them that their services were no longer needed. The people began to take their leave, crowding around the door she, her dad and the Shaman were also trying to go through. Being a large man, U stood in front of the other guests, blocking their passage, so his group to exit first without having their space invaded. Dee saw the faces of the other guests, and they were not pleased with U at all. Dee slept on the ride back and didn't wake until they arrived at the hotel. Solomon put her to bed, and the Shaman brought her a mineral tonic to drink before she fell asleep.

The next evening, Dee woke to see the three men in her room, all anxious to see how she was doing and hear about her visit with the royal lady. "I'm hungry," she said. "I knew helping the lady would be hard." The Shaman said, "It's a good sign that she's hungry." Solomon told her to wash up, and they would eat dinner downstairs. She hadn't realized she had slept right through the day and missed not only breakfast but lunch as well.

The hotel dining room was crowded, but there was a table available for them. The group ordered their meal and ate at their leisure. Afterwards, the maître d' asked them to please remain seated, as they were to receive a special visit from a royal. He then announced to the remaining patrons that they would have to leave the dining room immediately. The other diners were not happy about this and complained; some hadn't even had a chance to finish their meals. The maître d' then announced that their meals were free of charge and that arrangements had been made for those who had been displaced to have a free driving tour of the palace of the royal family. The vans were waiting for them outside. Their feelings of discontent were forgotten, as they made their way from the dining room outside to the vans. One of the guests stopped at Solomon's table on his way out, urging them to hurry before all the vans filled. When she heard this, Dee said to her dad, "I don't want to go back to the castle." Solomon assured her that they weren't going back.

In spite of the free tour and the dinners, there were still stragglers in the dining room. The maître d' and the staff attempted to rush people out, but one table was intent on staying and finishing their meal in their own time. This came to an abrupt end when four Royal Guards entered and told them to leave immediately. No further words were spoken, and the reluctant patrons left the area.

The dining room was quiet, as Solomon's table was the only one occupied. The Royal Guards took up positions around the room. The lady Dee had helped to sleep now entered the room accompanied by six Royal Guards. U was out of his seat in an instant and stood behind Dee. Solomon told him to relax and stand firm. Two employees of the hotel arrived with a special chair for the lady to sit in. The lady sat and smiled at the group, then reached out her hand for Dee, who recoiled and went to sit on her father's lap. The lady thanked Solomon for his help and requested permission to hold the child for a moment. He accepted her gratitude but refused to allow her to hold his daughter. The lady accepted that and thanked him again.

She then raised her hand, and a man in her entourage reached into a briefcase and retrieved a black folder embossed with gold and silver letters, which he passed to Solomon. While the royal lady and Solomon were engaged in conversation, Dee asked the Shaman for something to drink. He prepared another elixir for her, made with brown powder and water.

The lady raised her hand again, motioning to one of her entourage to place a large gift basket on the table near Dee. The little girl leaned over to examine the contents. The lady said, "It's filled with exotic fresh fruits from all around the world." She wanted to give them something extra because she had slept for thirteen hours straight. "I haven't slept that soundly since I was a child!" she announced joyfully.

She seemed very grateful and happy, so Dee took the opportunity to ask her about the tall man she had been dancing with in her dream. The lady was caught completely off guard by the question and knocked a glass near her off the table. U managed to catch it before it hit the floor. Then the lady told her guards and entourage to leave the room. They were reluctant but obeyed her wishes.

When they had left, the lady turned and asked Dee, "How did you know about the tall man?" Dee looked to her dad before answering, and he gave a nod of approval.

"I saw the beginning of your dream when the man came to dance with you."

"How were you able to see my dream?" the lady asked.

"I can't explain how I did it. I only know what I saw," replied Dee.

The woman smiled affectionately and said. "You have an extraordinary child, would it be okay if I gave her a hug."

"I don't want to be hugged because it will make me tired again and I want to play later," said Dee.

"You have your answer," Solomon told the lady.

The lady then lifted her hand, motioning for one of her guards to assist her from the chair, but since they were not in the room, U helped her. She stood up and told Solomon, "If you ever return to my country again, I would be honored to have all of you as guests in my home." She turned to leave, followed by her entourage, who were back inside the room. U stayed to watch them leave, while Solomon, Dee, and the Shaman returned to their room.

Dee asked her father, "Why did all the people in the restaurant have to leave?" He explained that the lady was an important person with ties to the royal family, so precautions had to be taken to assure her safety. Soon there was a knock at the door. U answered and saw two Royal Guards. One of them handed U a black pouch, then they both left without saying a word. U closed the door and gave the pouch to Solomon. Inside was a note sealed with red wax. It read: "This is for your man who graciously helped me out of my chair."

Solomon emptied the contents of the pouch on the table: It was a stack of money wrapped in paper and a single gold coin. He replaced the items without looking any further and returned the pouch to U.

"I can't accept this," protested U. "You have done so much for me; how can I accept this?"

"Nonsense," said Solomon. "It was a gift for you, and you wouldn't want to offend the lady, would you?"

U hesitated, but eventually took the pouch and placed it in his suitcase. Dee went to bed, and the next morning, the four of them left for home.

Ancient Cave

Solomon traveled to Virginia and spoke with some men about an ancient cave that had been discovered. It had been sealed for many years without any way to safely gain access. It was situated inside a mountain bordered by the ocean, and it was believed that the sea water had severely eroded the walls. Because of this, blasting it open was not an option, as this would most likely cause the whole structure to fall in on itself. Solomon told the men that he might be willing to try to open the cave for them. In turn, they spoke excitedly with their director, who then had a further discussion with Solomon in private. In the end, it was agreed that Solomon would be sent to the cave to see what he could do.

Solomon arrived home early the next morning, and Dee ran to hug him as she jumped into his arms. He smiled and gave her a hug and kissed her mom. "I won't be home for long," he said. "I have to leave again late tonight." Ella was concerned that he was traveling too much, but he reassured her that he would be fine. "I'll be meeting U later, and Dee is coming along," he said. Dee was overjoyed and ran to her room to get her little suitcase ready. This time her mom didn't complain about her traveling with her dad.

"You better get some rest before you have to leave again," her mom advised.

"You're right, Ella," he said.

Solomon slept until late in the evening, and when he got up, they prepared themselves for the trip.

They left for the airport and spotted U already at the terminal. "Hello, Little D!" U exclaimed as he reached down to pick her up. As they walked through the airport, Solomon briefed U on the trip. "We will be traveling on a government plane with scientists and military personnel," he said. "They found mysterious ancient cave years ago and have been unable to safely gain access to the interior."

"How did you find out about the cave?" U asked.

Solomon told him all about his visit to Virginia and said, "I offered my assistance, but not without a few favors in return."

"This is going to be an interesting trip," U chuckled, and Solomon agreed.

They boarded a flight that took them to the departure location of the government plane. Dee was taken by surprise at the size of it. Military personnel and teams of scientists were on board, and they even had two flight attendants serving food and drinks. Solomon's group were the only people of color on board, and one of the soldiers seemed to have an issue with U and had fixed his eyes on him with a cold stare. U stared back. The commanding officer noticed the exchange and ordered all his troops to the back of the plane for the duration of the flight.

On arrival, the soldiers grabbed their gear and were the first to exit the plane. The commanding officer ordered some of them to ready the boat for the following morning, where they would be on standby near the back of the cave. As for everyone else, they would be going to the campsite that had been established not far from the cave entrance.

The trio were preparing to disembark when a scientist approached Solomon and said, "We'll be waiting in the hanger until transportation arrives to take us to the campsite." There were two teams of scientists on site: one from the United States and the other from Denmark. The scientist that had approached Solomon was with the American team, and he had given Solomon maps to study. They waited in groups: the scientists in two separate groups and the remaining soldiers in another group with their commanding officer. Dee, her father and U were sitting together.

A Danish scientist approached the American team and asked a question in a low voice. One of the American scientists spoke loudly and proclaimed that he was the leader of the expedition. When the commander heard, he immediately corrected the American scientist by making it clear that he was in charge, and nothing would be done without his permission.

"That's just like those military types," the scientist said in response, "to take over our projects without any scientific expertise." Then he turned back to his group to study his maps.

Solomon observing this behavior said, "I'll be glad when we get this over with."

The trucks finally arrived, and everything was loaded up and they were off. When they arrived at the campsite, and the soldier who had stared U down on the plane approached Solomon. U stepped between them and stood face to face with the soldier.

"You will have to speak to me. Never speak directly to Mr. Solomon," he demanded.

The soldier looked back at the commander who was observing for direction. The commander nodded. The soldier advised U where he and the others would be housed at the campsite. It was a blue and black tent at the other end of the camp. The tent was sparse and included three cots, a metal box, a small chair and two backpacks.

Once inside, Solomon sat on a cot reviewing his maps and told Dee to take the other cot. U said he wanted to walk around the campsite to check everything out. Before he left, Dee asked him to wait. Then she walked around him and adjusted his energy. "Your energy needed fixing, Uncle U," said Dee. He thanked her and stepped out of the tent. U returned a short time later and informed Solomon about the layout of the camp site.

Just then, a soldier called to them from outside their tent. "Mr. Solomon's presence is required in the commander's tent, and I am here to escort you there." Solomon stepped out with Dee and U and said, "Lead the way." The soldier took them to the commander's tent. Once inside, Solomon offered Dee a chair and sat down next to her, while U remained standing behind them. Both scientist teams were seated near the commanding officer, who began briefing everyone on the safety requirements and procedures they would have to follow.

Then the commander said, "If anyone has a fear of tight spaces or darkness, let me know now, and you will not be included in this expedition." He continued, "I don't have any patience or time to deal with those particular issues." He looked directly at each person in the tent, and no one spoke up. He then looked over to Solomon and Dee. "Will the little girl be okay?" he asked. Solomon stood up and replied, "My daughter does not have those issues, as you call them." The CO accepted Solomon's words and the briefing continued.

The commander gave a report on the previous failed attempts to open the cave last month and said they would try three more times tomorrow with the three teams present. The Danish team would begin, and if they failed, Solomon and his team would make the second effort. If they failed, the

American team would be the last to try. One scientist from the Danish team seemed to be upset by Dee's presence.

"Why is this young child involved with this project?" the Danish scientist asked. "This is a significant discovery, and we shouldn't be bothered by the presence of a kid."

Before allowing the commanding officer to respond, an American scientist asked, "Exactly how is this little girl relevant to a discovery of this nature?" The commander drew the inquiries to a halt. "Mr. Solomon and his team were invited by the Director of the XXX. If he and his team fail to open the cave, they will immediately be escorted off the site and sent home. The same course of action will apply to any team that fails."

The CO advised the scientists not to worry about anything other than their purpose for being dispatched to the site. "Over the past years there have been many attempts to open the cave, and all have failed," he said. "I've been on this mission for a long time, and they won't allow me to blow the damn thing open." He dismissed everyone to their sleeping quarters and advised them to get some rest. The next day they would start before sunrise with the Danish team.

The meeting ended, and Solomon, U, and Dee returned to their tent. Dee announced that she would sleep through the night and didn't want to get up unless it was absolutely necessary. Then she crawled into her cot, while Solomon busied himself studying the maps. As Dee began drifting off to sleep, she heard them talking about the wonders that might be discovered inside the cave.

The following morning, Dee woke up early and her dad gave her something to eat and tried to fix her hair the best he could. They went outside the tent and saw a few soldiers headed to the cave site. U had gotten up extra early to tag along with the Danish team when it was their turn. He wanted to see what methods they would use in their efforts to open the cave. Dee walked back inside and lay on her cot.

"You don't want to see how the scientists attempt to open the cave?" Solomon asked.

"The Danish team will not be able to open it," Dee advised.

"How do you know?" Solomon asked.

"The scientists don't know how to move the stones."

Since they had not yet gone to the cave site, her dad didn't know anything about the 'stones' she was talking about.

"What stones, Dee? How do you know about them?"

"I saw the stones in my dreams last night, and I know I can open the cave when it's our turn," she replied.

Solomon looked at his daughter with a smile on his face and said, "Okay, Little D, you just get some rest."

Soon after, U returned from his trip to the cave site and reported to Solomon. The commander would not allow anyone to get close to the cave's entrance except the Danish scientists. So he had been unable to see their chosen strategy. The commander had stayed with the team for 30 minutes in a makeshift covered area. When he left the scientists this morning, he seemed irate and complained about having to complete another tour of duty on the mission.

"While I was in Virginia, I heard of other more risky options for opening the cave being discussed," said Solomon. "Well, Little D, it looks like you're the one who is going to open it for them."

"Only if you want me to, Dad," she replied.

Dee went to sleep, and several hours later she heard voices outside the tent. She got out of her cot and peeked outside. The commander, a Danish scientist, Solomon, and U were talking. The scientist was pleading with Solomon to forfeit some of his team's time to allow extra time for his team's efforts. The commander had already declined the request, but the Danish team leader was trying to circumvent his authority by speaking directly to Solomon. However, Solomon would not allow them to have any of his allotted time.

It was at this moment that Dee intervened. She stepped out into the afternoon sun to stand quietly next to her father. He kneeled at her level to hear what she had to say. Everyone was quiet as she whispered in his ear. She was asking Solomon to give the Danish team some of their time because she didn't require much to open the cave.

Then Solomon told the commander. "It's okay; give them some of our time." The commander rejected the idea, telling Solomon and the scientist that they had already been thoroughly briefed on the procedures last night. He further explained that when the project had started years ago, each team had been allotted two days to open the cave. The time had since been scaled back with each failed series of attempts. Past experience showed that if they were not able to open the cave with the restrictions that had been put in place within the first few hours, it was more than likely that they never would. Therefore, the commander could not and would not grant the Danish team more time.

The Danish team was instructed to pack up their equipment, and they would be escorted off the site. The CO then asked Solomon if he was ready to go. Solomon said he needed a few minutes. He and Dee readied themselves for the task before walking up the mountain. Soldiers were standing with the team of American scientists at a distance from the cave opening. They walked past them and arrived at the cave entrance. The commander said that they had eight hours and he would remain with them for the first 30 minutes as was his custom. He asked that he be notified immediately if they decided to give up so that the next team could begin.

Dee stood at the cave entrance gazing at it for several minutes as Solomon and U watched patiently. The commander soon got up from his viewing position and left them to their work without even waiting the full 30 minutes as he had promised. At this point, Dee instructed her father and U to push into the rocks that she pointed out while she touched their elbows. She then instructed U to move a tree branch out from under the rock nearest him. When this was done, they all stood back because small rocks and sand began falling, creating a cloud of dust.

When the dust cleared, three images could be seen on the cave entrance that had not been visible before. They were of three triangles, and two of them were positioned with points facing downwards, while the third was pointing upward. One of the outer triangles had squiggly lines above it and the second had tiny circles above it. The center triangle had a line with a small circle above it. Dee knew that the triangle's orientation had to be changed to safely gain access to the cave.

Solomon sent U to retrieve the commander so he would be present when the cave opened. The commander was already on his way back to the entrance and spotted U.

"Is everyone all right? I saw the dust cloud!" he shouted.

"We're all right and ready to open the cave," said U.

The commander slowed his stride, and he and the soldiers with him broke out into laughter. They knew that this second group had been at the cave entrance less than 30 minutes.

"It's not open yet, but perhaps you would like to see the symbols that have become visible," said U.

The CO stopped laughing. "What symbols?" he asked. "There aren't any symbols at the entrance!"

He then ordered one of the soldiers to get the photographer, and they picked up their pace towards the cave.

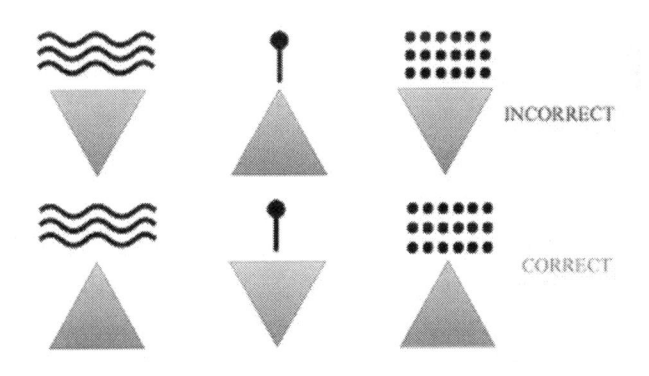

Cave Symbols

Dee and Solomon had been examining the images as they waited for the CO to arrive. The commander was incredulous when he saw the symbols. "How were they discovered?" he asked. Solomon evaded the question. "We were just waiting for you before we open it," he said. The photographer arrived out of breath and began to snap pictures of the symbols. Solomon and U turned to keep an eye on the photographer. The commander said, "Everything has to be photographed and documented so that the mission can be accurately reported and cataloged." He turned to another soldier and said, "Go notify Virginia with a situation report." The soldier headed quickly back to the camp.

The photographer turned his camera towards Dee and Solomon, but U covered the lens. "No photos will be taken of us," Solomon instructed.

"Photos have to be taken; it's part of the procedure," the commander interjected.

"That was not part of our agreement," Solomon advised.

"Are you sure you can open the cave?" The CO asked. Solomon assured him that they could. Then the CO ordered the photographer not to take any photos of Solomon and his team.

Dee instructed everyone to move back because there would be a rockslide when the cave entrance opened. Until that moment, it had never occurred to the CO that Dee would be responsible for opening the cave. He had assumed it would be Solomon. He reminded Solomon that he could not and would not be responsible for the child's safety. "Only I am responsible for my daughter," Solomon assured him. Then everyone stepped back. Dee remained at the cave entrance alone. She placed an energy shield around herself to protect herself from the rocks and debris that would fall. She checked behind her to make sure everyone was a safe distance away. Then she examined the symbols and closed her eyes for a moment. She waved her right hand across the triangle with the circles, and it turned clockwise. She waved her left hand across the triangle with the squiggly lines, causing it to turn as well. She then waved her hand over the center triangle and increased the energy inside, then placed both hands on it as she began pushing it into the wall.

It took less than a minute, and rocks began breaking away from the top of the entrance and crashed down around her. As the debris rained down, Dee was obscured from the others by a huge cloud of dust. But she could still see that everyone was trying to get to her, so she yelled at them to stay back because the rocks were still falling. U continued trying to get to her anyway. "Stay back! I'm okay, Uncle U!" she yelled. "If anyone comes too close, the cave will close again!"

Everyone waited impatiently until she gave the all clear. The CO was the first to reach the cave entrance. He stopped in front of Dee and saw the big pile of rocks all around her.

"Who are you and where did you come from?" asked the CO. "How did you not get crushed by all the falling rocks?"

Dee didn't respond and looked to Solomon, who replied, "We're here to open the cave, not answer your questions."

The photographer used the distraction to attempt to take another photo of them. U stepped in his path and told the CO, "Next time your photographer tries taking a photo of us, I'm going to break his camera." The CO looked at U and the photographer. "Settle down, men," he said. Then he directed his soldiers to bring the lights so they could begin their exploration of the cave.

One of the American scientists had already been busy taking soil samples and performing quick field tests. He reported that the walls of the cave were not very safe, based on his preliminary tests. But the commander disregarded his warning and ordered his soldiers to run the lights through to the next cavern. Before entering, Dee told her dad not to touch any of the triangle shapes on the wall or floors because they were traps. He relayed the information to the CO, who in turn told his troops.

However, the information did not disseminate quickly enough to the troops who were ahead setting up the lights. One of those soldiers leaned up against the wall, pushing on one of the triangles. The ground below him opened up, and he fell straight through it. When the CO and U arrived to help, the scene below was gruesome. The hole had opened to reveal a sharp stalactite rock that had penetrated the soldier's body.

The commander paused looking at the soldier's body down below. Then he got right back to business, cautioning his troops again to watch for the triangular shapes. Dee needed to enter the next cavern alone, explaining that it was infested with large spiders and she would have to return them to their nest before anyone could enter. Upon hearing this, the CO said, "I have flame throwers and could just as easily burn them."

Dee quietly cautioned her dad against killing the spiders. "It will make all the walls come down," she said. Solomon informed the CO and said, "Killing the spiders will destabilize the already tenuous structure of the walls, causing them to collapse and crush us all. If you feel that you or any of your men could get the spiders back into their nest, or if you want to kill them, then you are welcome to try while we wait outside." The commander threw up his hands in resignation and stepped aside.

There was another triangle partially obscured by dust on the floor near the entrance to the next cavern. Dee pointed it out to the others and told them not to touch it, or the cave entrance would close. The commander ordered one soldier to remain as a sentry outside the entrance as a precaution. He then invited the American scientist who had been taking samples to have a look inside the cavern. Neither had ever seen spiders quite so large.

The CO then permitted Solomon to proceed, while he and the scientist watched Dee go into the next cavern. Dee moved the webs away from her as she moved to the middle of the room where the largest spiders were located. Solomon and U were at the entrance watching her, and behind them stood the others, also peering in. She closed her eyes and began to vibrate, causing the spiders to crawl onto her. Soon her whole body was completely covered with them. She found her way to the hole where their nest lay.

U seemed amazed and proud of Dee. He placed a hand on her dad's shoulder and said, "The spiders love her, Solomon!" Once again, the photographer tried to take a photo of Dee, but U grabbed the camera and threw it into the hole where the soldier had fallen. The commander attempted to intercept it, but he was too late.

The commander rushed back to the cavern entrance in time to see the amazing spectacle of Dee and the spiders. Dee was aware of everything going on around her and still was able to focus on her task. She was standing near the wall, her skin emanating a blue light of energy. She raised her hand into the hole, and the spiders began to crawl from her body back into their nest. After she had removed her arm from the nest, the last spider turned toward her, and instantly she remembered seeing it in her dreams the night before.

Dee shut down her energy field, hiding her light from view. U and Solomon began to make their way to her, and she cautioned them to watch out, as there was another triangle covered with a thick layer of dust in their path. They stepped over the triangle and began wiping the cobwebs off her. The CO and the last soldier followed in Solomon's footsteps avoiding the triangle. The photographer had inadvertently stepped on one of the triangles with the side of his foot. His misstep caused a heavy rumbling to emanate from the depths of the cave. Everyone ran toward the entrance as it began to close. The sentry outside struggled to keep the cave entrance open. The photographer was the closest to the exit and ran desperately to escape. Dee yelled at the sentry, "Get out of the way!" But it was too late. The cave's entrance closed, and the sentry was crushed beneath its massive weight. The photographer stood only a few feet from the closed exit, frozen in fear.

All of a sudden, another large boulder fell from above, crushing the photographer in an instant. When the dust settled, the commander and the last soldier in the cave wiped away human debris and blood from their uniforms. The scientist screamed in panic. "What should we do now? We're trapped with no way out!" U heard a scratching sound and asked if the soldier had a radio. The soldier tried to hand the radio to the CO, but the scientist grabbed it, frantically attempting to call for help. The commander took the radio from him and announced, "This is Commander Lincoln OLSD18 on site. Is anyone there?" A soldier's voice came over the waves. "We read you and heard what happened. Is everyone accounted for?" The commander delivered the site report and said, "We lost three men."

The soldier informed the commander that the outer walls of the cave were crumbling and had begun to fall into the ocean below. But they could see that there was another opening to the cave that had been created in the cliffs. Everyone trapped in the cave would have to get to that opening to avoid the collapse. The scientist went into a frenzy. The commander slapped his face. "Pull yourself together, man!" he demanded. "Look at this child – is she panicking or fearful?"

"Well, we all know that's not a normal child," the scientist replied, looking sideways to Dee. Solomon did not take kindly to his comment and warned that he'd do well to keep his words to himself.

The soldier stated that he had heard water flowing below them earlier, and advised them to follow it to lead them to the opening in the cliff. He was sent on a reconnaissance mission, while everyone else took a moment to drink water and collect themselves. The scientist refused to share the canteen that was passed around to Solomon and Dee. The commander had his own canteen and took a drink from it before passing it to the scientist.

The group was quiet as Dee listened for the sound of the water. Soon she yelled out, "Hey! I hear water." The others strained to listen to the flow of water but were unsuccessful. Dee asked her father to direct the men to follow her as quietly as possible so that she might follow the sound of the water. They followed her, moving carefully and avoiding any other triangle. She turned to whisper to her dad that she could see the energy of the water through the walls. Solomon was coughing from the dust in the damp musty cave, and she noticed for the first time that he looked incredibly old and tired. She wondered if he should even be in the cave, and questioned why he had even agreed to go.

U offered the canteen to Solomon so that he could take a drink. The scientist complained that they shouldn't stop because they were surely running out of time. U urged the scientist to remain silent. The soldier that had been sent ahead for reconnaissance returned and found them. He had followed the sound of the water which led to two tunnels, but he was unable to determine which one led to the outside. They quickly and carefully followed the soldier to where the tunnels split. Dee told her father that they would need to take the path to the left.

The CO followed their directions, and after walking a while, he asked, "Are you sure we took the right path?"

"I will be following my daughter. You are all welcome to turn back and take the other path if you choose, Solomon replied."

They all continued to follow Dee, and after a short time, they came to a dead end. The scientist was upset.

"We took the wrong path following this child, and we must go back before it's too late," he said.

"He is right," the commander calmly told Solomon. "We will have to turn around and try the other path."

Her dad bent down to Dee and asked for instructions.

"We must continue following this path, or we won't make it out," was her reply.

The path dead-ended at a wall that had a medium-sized breach about five feet above the ground. Dee, using her abilities and senses, advised her father that they would be able to continue to follow the path by going through the opening in the wall. It would lead to yet another opening where they would see the light.

Solomon relayed the message to the men behind them, adding that if they chose to go back, they would never make it out. The commander thought about their options. Solomon suggested that he place his head in the hole in an attempt to hear the waves splashing against the rocks below. The commander, who was as big as U, climbed all the way into the hole which was just large enough for him to fit. As he listened to the water, Dee told

Solomon that they had to leave immediately. Just then, the cave began to rumble again. The trembling caused the CO to depart quickly from the hole. His voice echoed off the tunnel walls as he announced, "This is the path we're taking!"

The soldier volunteered to go first for recon but was told there wasn't enough time. Solomon climbed into the opening first as U lifted Dee up and then followed her inside. Then the scientist crawled in, followed by the CO and the soldier. The scientist, true to his negative self-serving ways urged Solomon to go faster before they were all crushed.

Solomon reached the cave opening below, and dropped down and held out his arms for Dee. U jumped down with the grace of a gymnast, but the scientist fell out of the hole and hurt his ankle. Just as the commander and soldier dropped down from the hole, a large rock fell from inside and sealed it shut. The scientist hobbled toward the sunlight screaming, "I can see the ocean and the soldiers in a boat below!"

The soldier was already busy fabricating a makeshift zip line that would carry them down to the ocean. Dee touched Uncle U's leg and told him to grab the scientist's shirt quickly. U did so without hesitation. The scientist was startled and misinterpreted U's action as aggression until the ledge he was standing on gave way beneath him. U held the screaming scientist by his shirt while he dangled from the cliff. The soldier rushed to help, but U pulled him up with help from a strong gust of wind. The scientist was finally rendered speechless.

The commander laughed. "You have nothing to say now." Then the commander contacted the boat captain on the radio. They saw the mountain crumbling into the ocean. "I'm not sure how long the zip line will hold," said the soldier. The scientist stepped forward. "I can't swim, and I'm injured." The commander radioed the boat, informing them of the situation, and assured the scientist he would be assisted once in the water.

The zip line and harness that the soldier made was ready, and at Solomon's request, the injured scientist was to go first. U helped the soldier harness the scientist, and he screamed all the way down. When he hit the water the soldiers assisted him onto the boat. Solomon requested that the commander go next, but he had to wait for approval from his superiors. It soon came by way of the radio. He made it to the water with ease and swam to the boat on his own. Dee and her father were next, and because she was so small, they would go together. The soldier asked U if he had had any specialized training jumping into the water and U replied that he did. U and the soldier jumped in the ocean together just as they released Solomon and Dee. The soldier and U made it with ease, but Solomon and Dee had a problem.

The zip line lost its anchor, and Solomon and Dee began to slide roughly down the mountain together. Solomon tried his best to slow them using his feet. Dee heard her dad's leg break as it became wedged between two rocks on a small outcropping on the cliff face where they stopped. Dee told Solomon she would heal his leg, but he instructed her not to for the moment. They looked below and saw U and the soldier in the water. The soldier was swimming to the boat, but U remained in the water looking up at Solomon and Dee. Her dad directed her to stand on the edge of the cliff, and jump into the water where U would help her. But she refused and said, "I won't go without you."

With that, she placed one hand on the side of the cliff, and, using her magick, freed her father's foot from the rocks. She then told him to hold on tight because she could feel an intense energy flowing through her. The mountain began to shake as Dee used her powers to change a rough path that led to the ocean into a smooth rock slide going directly into the water. The soldiers on the boat were looking up as she did her magick in the open, but she didn't pay them any mind. Her only concern was getting her father off the cliff and out of danger.

Dee told her dad to lean back to begin the slide down the mountain. He looked down and saw that the slide was heading straight into the water. He cautioned her about it. Using her powers again, Dee touched the rock slide, and it began curling up at the end. They began their descent, sliding down to the water like two kids on a water slide at an amusement park. Dee was smiling all the way down until they hit the water. U swam to her and placed one of the floatation devices around her. Then he began to swim to her father. Solomon waved him off and courageously swam to the boat on his own, broken foot and all.

Once on board, U dropped to his knees apologizing for having jumped before seeing to their safety.

"Get up," said Solomon. "No apology is necessary; you're an honorable man."

Dee had never seen U so emotional.

"None of these people are worthy to be in you and your daughter's presence, least of all me."

"Nonsense, you have always been true and worthy," said Solomon.

Dee hugged Uncle U, and he picked her up and handed her right back to her dad.

"I will go last from now on," said U.

"This may be our last trip, so you won't have to worry about that anymore," Solomon advised him.

Dee requested that U shield her with a blanket to block the others from seeing her heal her father's leg. She felt an intense energy within her, and as soon as she touched the broken leg, it was healed. The commander approached Solomon. "The director would like to meet with you as soon as possible," he said. Solomon acknowledged the request, and the commander saluted him and Dee before returning to his seat. The other soldiers were all whispering amongst each other while looking over at Dee.

Back at home, Solomon, who was over sixty years old, said he could not do any more favors for 'them.' His body had already been through too much in life, but it had all been done for the benefit of his special child. He was relieved that they had accomplished what they had set out to do and that all requirements for the mystery school admission had finally been met. Dee had now assured herself of an invitation to all six mystery schools, as well as a place for another person of her choice. They had made this great achievement just in time, as old age had truly caught up with her father.

Dee was taken back home, and Solomon left the next day for a debriefing with the director. He was gone for only a day, and when he returned, Dee followed him to his room. She saw him place his journal on his bed as he began unpacking. Dee knew the journal was significant to him because he always kept it near him. When Solomon went to the kitchen to get a drink of water, she began looking through all the pages. She saw lots of notes, signatures, and statements her father had gotten from many people over the years. She also noticed that her dad had received a signature from the Director of the ___. It was the last entry in the book. It is believed that Solomon recorded the favors owed and promises made in his journal.

Visiting Wild Animals: The Black Panther

It was October of 1971 and Dee was almost six years old. She had received invitations to attend all six secret mystery schools and would begin the first school in 1977. Her potential was limitless and her power immense. She still wanted to be at her best and learn the hidden knowledge that only the mystery schools offered. This is what she and her father had tirelessly worked so hard for and finally gained. Not only were they awarded invitations to attend the mystery schools, but Dee was given the opportunity to choose a partner to attend the schools with her. This was quite an achievement, and extremely rare considering the schools only invited a few students per year. Dee was destined to be a force for good in the world.

Dee's only other desire was to be among wild animals. She told Solomon about a vision she had as a one-year-old baby. It was one of her very first visions, and she was in the presence of what seemed to be every animal in the world. There were many different animals, and she had never seen most of them. The animals had an energy and purpose that was truer to their nature than was the case with humans, and it made her feel good being around them. The energy of most people she encountered was highly negative, and she knew this from feeling their deepest desires.

Solomon recognized Dee's wish and made arrangements for them to go on safaris around the world. The first trip they took was to Africa, and Dee had no idea what part they went to because she was only a child. After a very long flight, they arrived at their destination, and a tall, dark-skinned man greeted Solomon. He loaded their bags into a truck and drove them to his village. As they drove down the dirt roads, Dee saw people striding along carrying loads under their arms or on top of their heads.

They came upon a remote village, and native children ran up to play with her. Dee looked at her dad for approval, and with his nod, she ran off with the other children, while Solomon went to speak with the village elders. When her father had finished, Dee ran back to him. She saw two village men in clothing unlike the rest of the villagers. They wore beige cargo pants with matching button-down shirts. Solomon said they would be their guides, and the man who had met them at the airport would be their driver and translator.

Other village men were setting up a tent for them, while their guides loaded additional supplies on the truck. The driver approached Solomon.

"We will be leaving at dawn," he said.

"Can I follow the children to the river?" asked Dee.

"Yes, but be careful," her dad replied.

Two village girls bounded towards Dee and took hold of her hands to lead her to the river with the other children. They all stopped a few steps from the river bank, and some boys went to pull some big green leaves from a bush. Then they gathered up some small pebbles and small brown leaves. They placed a brown leaf on top of the big green leaf and placed a pebble on top. They gently put each one into the river and watched them float away past the girls as they were soaking their hands and feet in the water.

Dee was led out the river, and the girls formed a circle around her. They wiggled their fingers while touching her upper body with their fingertips, chanting, "Is, Is, Is" over and over again. The boys formed an outer circle around the girls and sauntered towards them with their hands above their heads chanting, "Ra, Ra, Ra." The only word that came to Dee's mind was "love," so she began to chant, "Love, Love, Love." Soon they were all chanting "Is, Ra, Love." Then the girls wiggled their fingers down to her feet, and as they came back up, they stopped chanting, took two steps back and then sat on the ground. The boys shook their hands towards the girls' feet while chanting, then took two steps back and they sat down. Dee was still standing in the center of the two circles. She decided to turn a full circle while stretching out her arms, enveloping them within her energy. She looked up to the sky and shouted "Love," before sitting down.

Then the boys stretched out their arms, touching each other's shoulders as they leaned from right to left. The girls did the same thing, except they moved from left to right, alternating with the boys. All the children were moving in sync with one another. Dee started moving her arms up to the sky, then back down to the ground. They began singing, and Dee shouted "Love!" The boys shouted "Ra!" and the girls shouted "Is!" At the end, they all put their hands up to the sky and blew kisses at the sun while jumping and laughing.

Then a woman called for the children, and they all ran back to the village. Dee saw her dad and ran over to tell him about the fun she had with the village children. The next morning, they left the village for the safari with the two guides and the driver. The drive was long and bumpy, and Dee and her dad held on tight.

They drove until they arrived at a path that led into the jungle. "We'll have to continue on foot from here," said the driver. They unhitched their packs from the truck, slung them over their shoulders, and began the trek into the jungle. Solomon was over sixty years old, but both he and Dee were able to keep up with the young guides.

The party walked until it was almost dark. Then the driver said, "We should make camp here before we lose the light." The men put up the tents and started a fire. "Go to bed when you finish eating," Solomon said to Dee. "We have a long day tomorrow." While Dee was eating, Solomon and the men talked. The driver was the only one who could speak English, and he had been acting as the translator. Dee tapped on her dad's arm and told him that she had to pee.

"Be careful; there are animals out hunting for food," the driver advised. "You're so small, one of them would not hesitate to eat you," he explained, with his clipped accent underscoring his serious look.

"I'm not scared," she said.

"Go behind the tree so I can keep an eye on you," said Solomon.

When Dee finished, she looked up and saw a tiny light at a distance in the bushes. She looked back and saw the men and her dad talking by the fire and not really paying attention to her. Dee began walking toward the light, and that one tiny light had become two. She took a few more steps. Her heart started thumping in her chest. Then without warning, a great big animal jumped and landed right in front of her. The animal's enchanting yellow eyes stared into her eyes, and she stared back.

By now Dee's heart was pounding so intensely that she could hear it, but she was not afraid. She held the animal's gaze for a minute, examining its unblinking eyes. She felt like blowing air into them just to make them blink. Then she felt her dad's energy surround her like a gust of wind and heard him tell the men not to move. One of them took aim with his rifle anyway, and she heard the click of the bolt. She looked back and saw that her dad held up his hand, warning the driver not to fire.

Dee turned back to the animal to get a better look at it and saw that it was a Black Panther. It was as tall as she was and as long as a Great Dane. The panther moved its attention from her and growled at Solomon and the men near the fire. The sound was so loud, she heard ringing in her ears and felt the moisture from the panther's hot breath wet her face.

"Focus, Little D, don't move," she heard her father say.

"I'm okay," she said unconcernedly. "It's growling at all of you, not me."

The panther gazed at Dee again, and she placed her small hand on its ear and started to rub it. She looked back and saw one of the men backing up. The panther moved its attention from her again and growled at the man.

"We need to shoot it before it kills her!" said the driver.

"Don't kill it!" Solomon advised.

Dee sensed the intense fear in the man with the rifle. The panther turned to her again, and she reached out and held its face with both hands while looking directly into its big yellow eyes. She put her little nose on its big black nose and rubbed behind its ears. The panther made a noise and lay down. Dee climbed on its back to give it a hug. She could feel the panther's energy, and it felt very comforting. Before she could get off the animal's back, it stood up with her still on top. Dee began to rub the panther's neck to keep it calm. She held on tightly with one hand and her legs.

Her dad had a worried expression, so she smiled at him to let him know she was all right. When her dad saw that she was happy, he smiled back. The two guides dropped to their knees with their eyes and mouths wide open. Dee thought they looked really funny and chuckled in amusement.

The panther began to walk around the fire near the men and made a pass in front of her dad. It sniffed him, and Solomon stood very still as Dee reached up to touch him and ease his worry. Then the animal walked over to the guide holding the weapon. He was so afraid that he wet himself. The panther sniffed the man and quickly blew air from its nose directly at him. It then approached the other two men who were on their knees praying with their heads down. The panther sniffed them, and they didn't move an inch, too frightened to look up.

Solomon was now carefully walking behind the panther as it went towards the driver again, who was now praying with his eyes closed. "Just stay calm," Dee said. "It will pass you by." Solomon stopped near the driver and took the weapon out of his hands, carefully laying it on the ground. Dee continued to rub the Panther's ears as it walked around the fire three more times with her still on its back. It was late in the evening, and she was tired and began to yawn. The Black Panther lay down on its belly, and she got off its back. It stood up again and licked her face with its large wet tongue.

Dee looked up and saw the driver bend down toward the weapon her dad had laid on the ground. The panther let out a deep growl, and the driver froze in his bent position as light from the fire danced in its eyes. Dee placed her hand on the panther's head, and the growling subsided. The panther looked at her once again, crouched on all fours and sprang away, disappearing into the darkness. Dee lay down on the ground by the fire, and her dad picked her up. She woke up in the tent the next morning and saw her dad watching over her.

"Are you okay?" he asked.

"Yes, but do you remember the Black Panther?" she asked.

"I certainly do, and I will never forget it!" her father replied. "Now, let's pack up, we're leaving."

They began the long walk back to the truck. The driver asked Solomon if he wanted to rest, but he declined.

When they arrived at the village, the two guides went to speak with the elders. The driver went to a group of men, women, and children standing around a fire. Then many other villagers began gathering around the driver to listen to what he was saying. Soon, they all turned towards Dee and Solomon as they sat outside their tent.

"Can I go play with the children again?" she asked.

"Of course," her father replied.

Dee began skipping over to where the people were gathered. The driver stopped talking when he saw her approaching. Everyone turned to stare at her. The children that she'd been playing with earlier ran over to her, but not to play this time, they just wanted to touch her. Dee didn't like it, so she ran back over to her dad.

"Why do they only want to touch me and not play like before?" Dee asked.

"It's probably because the guide is telling everyone what happened with you and the Black Panther," Solomon explained.

A group of men was spotted bringing supplies to the village, and the driver rushed over to Solomon. "The grains, cows, and goats you arranged to be delivered have arrived," he said happily.

"Fantastic," said Solomon with a smile.

"I'm sure the elders would like to meet with you so they can express their gratitude for supplying us with so much."

"Of course," agreed Solomon.

He followed the driver inside to meet with the elders. Dee accompanied him since the children did not want to play with her anymore. Through the translator, the village elders asked Solomon to stay for another day. They were told what happen with the Black Panther and planned a great feast in their honor. They would also invite others from the neighboring villages to celebrate the grand occasion with them. Solomon agreed to stay. Ruffling Dee's hair, he said, "I'm tired from all the walking I've done and could use the rest."

After the meeting, they went back to their tent and slept for several hours. When they awoke, they could smell the aroma of cooked meat. After emerging from the tent, Dee saw many other villagers that she hadn't seen before. When she and Solomon were spotted, the people began to sing and dance in excitement. A group of women offered fruits and nuts to them. Then they joined the other villagers to feast.

The elders from all the villages sat next to Solomon and began a conversation through the translator. The children started to play with Dee again without trying to touch her like before, so she ran around with them while her dad was in conversation. They celebrated for most of the night, and Dee felt exhausted. They returned to their tent to sleep and prepare themselves for the trip back home.

The next morning, they'd packed their bags and went outside. Dee saw that all the villagers had gathered around their tent.

"Why are the people waiting outside our tent?" Dee asked.

"They are waiting to say goodbye to you," her father replied.

"Why do all the villagers want to say goodbye to me?"

"Because you are special and they know it."

After passing by all the villagers who were exalting his daughter, Solomon spoke to the elders one last time. Then they were escorted to the truck. The villagers rushed towards Dee trying to touch her. Solomon put her on his shoulders so they couldn't reach her and put her in the truck. They waved goodbye to the people as they drove away. "Your little girl and the Black Panther have brought luck to the villages!" said the driver while smiling. "Her story will be told for generations to come."

The driver dropped them off at a hotel and wished them happy journeys. Solomon and Dee left the hotel the next day for the airport. On the plane, Dee observed her dad writing in his journal before she drifted off.

Visiting Wild Animals: The Wolves

It was a bright sunny day. Dee was running around playing in the back yard by herself, holding her arms up as if she was going to take off and fly away. She stopped and fell to the grass on her back, closing her eyes. She astral projected out of her body, suddenly seeing the boy she dreamed of every night. Dee ran to him. He was, as usual, pleased to see her. They played at a wonderful playground they created together, inventing all sorts of fun things to do, sometimes playing the same games they had enjoyed together before.

In the midst of their games, the boy said, "I'll see you next time. Your father wants you to come back." They hugged each other and Dee heard her dad whisper her name. She opened her eyes and saw her father kneeling over her as she lay on the grass. He picked her up, and it felt to her as if she had slipped away from the boy's arms and into the arms of her father.

"Aw, Dad," she said with disappointment, "I was playing with the boy and having fun."

Solomon smiled. "Sorry, Dee, but it's almost time to visit with the wild animals again, and we have things to do before we leave."

"Yeah!" his daughter screamed in excitement.

"We're going to see wolves this time," Solomon said. "Wolves have heightened senses and are very smart, so we'll have to be extra careful on this trip. People have been severely hurt or killed by wolves because of carelessness."

Dee assured her father that everything would be okay, just as it was with the panther. Solomon kissed Dee on the cheek and sent her to Ella so she could get her hair washed and braided so she would look nice on her trip.

Thankfully, Ella no longer complained about Dee going on trips with her dad. Although she knew they were going on camping trips to see animals, Ella didn't realize how close they would get too wild animals. She thought they were going to an exotic zoo or wildlife reserve. She didn't know very much about any of the things her husband and daughter did when they traveled.

While her mom was washing her hair, Dee asked her to rinse it twice because the animals don't like the smell of soap. She remembered the panther trying to smell her through all the soap fragrances and then blowing air out of its nose. Her mom told her she was using a brown soap that the Shaman had given Solomon to use on her hair. It had a strange earthy smell. Her mom said the Shaman probably made it from some of the trees and plants he grew.

When Dee's hair was done, her father came into her room. "Time to go to sleep, Little D," he said. "We'll be leaving before sunrise." Dee was ecstatic about going to sleep early because she would be able to visit with the boy again. She climbed into bed, and her dad tucked her in. "Have fun with the boy," he said. Ella was standing by the door listening in. "We should take her to a doctor. It isn't normal for a child to want to sleep so much," said Ella. "That's complete nonsense, Ella," said Solomon. "Besides, I just told her to go to bed early."

Solomon closed the door to her room, and Dee closed her eyes and went straight into the darkness – leaving her body in an instant. First, she saw stars all around her and then she saw the boy. He was standing between several doors lined up in a very long hallway. He waved at her to come over, and she ran to him. "Choose a door," said the boy, and she did. When they opened the door, they saw an infinite amount of dark empty space. The boy made a motion with his hand and illuminated the darkness of space. Then he made another motion with his hands and created a surface, as trees, grass, and flowers started to rapidly grow and stretch as far as their eyes could see. "Wow, I want to try," said Dee. So she waved her hand and created a sky that lit up space even more. With one more wave of her hand, an ocean was created, and the sounds of waves lapping at the shore filled their ears.

They continued creating the world the way they wanted it to be. Just as they were about to explore it further, the boy said, "Your mom is waking you up." Dee hugged the boy and waved goodbye before returning to her body. When she opened her eyes, Ella was dressing her. "Be quiet so that you won't wake Emma and Fred," her mom said, although they were in another room. Ella dressed her in the new camping clothes that Solomon purchased for her. "You look like a boy," Dee's mom said. "I don't know why your dad purchased this junk for you. You shouldn't wear clothing like this as a six-year-old girl."

Dee didn't say a word. She was still sleepy when her mom picked her up and put her in the front seat of the car. She went right back to sleep while her dad loaded the luggage in the trunk. The next time Dee woke, they were on a plane, and she saw that her dad was looking through his journal. She went right back to sleep again. She woke up again and was in her father's arms as they were walking from the plane into the airport terminal.

Solomon met the guide that he had hired to lead the safari. He was a middle-aged white man with long black hair, and he spoke English with an accent. The guide retrieved their bags and loaded them in his truck, and after a long drive, they arrived at a fenced-in area. Dee saw another man wearing a brown uniform with a badge approaching them, and the guide went to speak with him. After a while, the uniformed man came up to Solomon and asked for his passport. After slowly examining the pages, the man gave it back. Then the guide reached into his bag and gave the man an envelope with money inside.

"Remember," the man in uniform said to Solomon, "no animal is to be harmed unless someone's life is in danger."

Solomon gave a slight nod. "Of course, we came to see the animals, not kill them."

"You should leave your daughter, sir," he said, gesturing toward Dee. "The wolves would have no problem eating a small child."

"She'll be by my side at all times," Solomon said, draping an arm around Dee and squeezing her close to him.

Soon they were on their way, driving through a long trail in the jungle. Dee could sense the eyes of different animals peering at them as they passed by.

Their arrival at the campsite was just before dark. Two other guides were sitting by a fire in front of three tents. Two small and one large, and all of them were different colors. The leader told Solomon that the large tent was for him and his daughter. As they unloaded their bags, Dee asked her dad why their tent was much nicer than the other two. "It should be nicer," he replied. "I paid for everything."

Once settled inside, Dee and Solomon stepped out to join the other men at the fire. But when the men saw them, they began whispering to each other and staring at the pair, so Solomon changed his mind about joining them.

That's when the leader called them over to his tent and showed Solomon some guns and strange looking ammunition.

"Do you know how to use these weapons?" the leader asked.

"Yes, I'm familiar with them," Solomon replied.

"Great!" he said. "I suspect you heard my men complaining. They don't understand why you brought a child out here. But don't worry; they will do their job."

"What exactly is their job?" Solomon asked.

"Two of the men are responsible for putting up the cages and security. One is a medic and animal expert, and there are three other men at a second site closer to the wolves who are also my assistants. Since you are familiar with some of the weapons, please go ahead and choose which one you want."

Solomon selected a pistol, and the guide gave him the tranquilizers to load. "I have just the thing for your daughter," he said while reaching for the sheath strapped to his chest. He pulled out a knife with an ivory handle that had a snake with blue eyes carved into it. He showed it to Dee, then put the knife back in the sheath, unstrapped it from his shoulder and instructed Solomon to strap it across Dee's shoulder and chest. Solomon did. Dee thanked the guide but said she would not need the knife. "Keep it anyway," he said. "It will make me feel better if you have it."

Dee turned to her dad, concerned. "The animals don't like guns! If they see them, they may not come around."

"Your daughter doesn't understand the dangers in the jungle," said the leader. "We will have to keep an eye on her at all times."

"She will be just fine, and I will be looking after her," replied Solomon.

The leader accepted this and began speaking about the cages they would build for themselves in case of an emergency.

"We will be miles away from the camp when we leave at dawn," he explained. "There are several wolf packs we've been recording information on. You must always listen to me when we are tracking the wolves. If I say it's time to go and you don't follow, my men and I will leave you for our own safety."

Solomon agreed and left with the weapon and ammunition.

Once in their tent, Dee asked her father if she could keep the ivory handled knife the leader had given her. "I don't know," he said. "It looks valuable, and he may not want to part with it. I will ask him when this is all over, but for now, it's time to sleep." Dee went to sleep without visiting the boy of her dreams. She listened to the animals making all sorts of noises. The wolves howled, and the other animals – even the insects – became quiet. After a while, she fell asleep.

The next morning after breakfast, the leader came over to their tent. "We're leaving in the next 30 minutes and should make it to the other campsite in about three hours." Static sounded from his radio, and one of his men began to speak. He was informed about a large pack of wolves in the old rock mount area that had left an injured cub inside a den. "We're leaving in a few minutes. Do not approach the den until I get there," he said.

"What is the old rock mount area?" Solomon asked.

"That's an old wolf den that the wolves have used before," he said. "Something happened to one of their cubs in the den, and they abandoned the location and moved on. When my men went inside to investigate years later, the only thing they found were the bones of dead wolves. They may have left the injured cub inside to die, but sometimes the female comes back to check on the cub so my men have to be careful."

The ride through the jungle was slow and bumpy, but it was a joyful day for Dee. She was excited that she was going to see another wild animal, and even happier to be with her dad, not to mention the shiny new knife she had strapped to her chest. They arrived at the second site where there was one big cage in the middle of the wilderness. A truck covered with branches and leaves was also on site. The guide pointed in the direction of the wolf den at the rock mount area and said it was less than a half hour walk away.

Solomon got out of the truck with Dee in his arms. The men stopped to stare at them and then began whispering to each other, just like the other men did the night before. The leader then gathered all his men around and spoke with them in private. When he was done, one of the men told Solomon to take Dee inside the cage. Then they put covers on the leader's truck, then bushes and leaves were put over the covers. One of the men told Solomon that everyone had to stay in the cage when the wolves were in the area. They had a lookout in a tree that would be the only person outside.

After a while, the man in the tree radioed the leader and reported that a pack of wolves was about five miles away. Solomon was asked if he wanted to see some photos of the wolves, which he was keen to do. Solomon viewed all the photos and then remarked, "The wolves look vicious and dangerous in some ways, but in other ways, they seem to be protecting their family and home." The man who gave him the photos agreed.

Another man brought over some of the bones that were retrieved from the old rock mount den years ago. He gave one to Dee, who immediately had a vision of the injured cub coming out of the den. She passed the bone to Solomon and asked, "Can we go see the wolf den?" The leader overheard her request and said, "Once we finish setting up the cages, we should have time to see it quickly." He and his men took more rifles and pistols from the leader's gun chest and hung them in the cage. "Let's go," he said, once everything was in place.

The leader and one of his men escorted Solomon and Dee to the den as they walked at a brisk pace. Dee saw the opening of the den, and let go of her dad's hand running towards it. The leader and Solomon yelled for her to wait, and she stopped in her tracks. "Go check it out," said the leader to his assistant. The assistant walked cautiously towards the den to investigate. He saw the wolf cub inside and poked it with his gun. It didn't move. "There's only a dying cub inside. It's all clear!" he yelled.

The leader gave the go ahead, so Solomon let Dee's hand go as she anxiously went inside. Her father waited outside, and the leader and guide stayed back as lookouts. Dee immediately saw the wolf cub and called for it. The cub awoke and walked toward her while dragging one of its legs. Dee had a piece of dried meat that one of the men had given her earlier, which her dad had told her to put in her pocket. She gave it to the cub, and it was quickly devoured. It licked her hand, and Dee decided to hug the cub and rub its injured leg. The cub growled in response.

Solomon heard the noise and called for Dee.

"The cub isn't dead. It's hurt and hungry," Dee responded.

The guide interjected, "Get her out of there! That cub might bite her!"

"Come back out!" yelled Solomon.

"Let me help the cub first, Dad!" she called back.

Dee rubbed her hands together until they turned a bright red color on the outside, with a blue glow in her palms. She held the cub in her arms and put her hands on its injured leg. She heard a crack from the cub's leg. It jumped out of her arms and ran around jumping up and licking her.

Dee got up to leave the cave now that the cub was healed. The cub trotted out ahead of her and past her dad.

"I thought you said the cub was dead," the guide said to his assistant.

"It must have been sleeping or playing dead," was the response.

The cub started to howl, and the leader told Solomon to pick up Dee so they could leave the area. The assistant climbed a tree to look around. He called down, "I see more wolves, and they're close! They turned when they heard the cub howl and are now headed towards us. We don't have time to make it back to the cage!" The assistant hurried down the tree to retrieve his rifle. "We have to take out the leader of the pack first," he said. But before he had a chance to climb back up the tree, two wolves he hadn't seen ran in front of him. Startled, he dropped his rifle and the camera he was carrying, and the camera shattered on a rock.

The wolves began growling at the man and were about to attack. Dee sensed he was in deep trouble and immediately placed a protective shield around him. Two more wolves approached her and Solomon, baring their fangs. The cub ran behind a rock near them and hid. Then a big black wolf appeared. It had shiny hair and a light brown color on his head, making it look as if he were wearing a crown. It crept behind the leader and began growling at him. The leader froze.

Dee was unafraid and put her hand out for the cub to come to her. The cub crept slowly from behind the rock and started to lick her hand. The big black wolf turned his attention away from the guide and growled at Solomon and Dee, showing his sharp fangs. The leader and his assistant still did not move an inch. Solomon also stood frozen.

The black wolf approached Dee, and she put her head closer to its mouth as it was growling. They locked gazes for a few seconds. The wolf huffed, and she could smell the blood on its breath and whiskers. The wolf's deep black eyes had a familiar look, and she realized they were the eyes of the boy from her dreams. So, she closed her eyes and kissed it on its big black nose, even as it was growling at her. The cub ran behind the black wolf and bit its tail, trying to pull it away from Dee.

The wolf kicked the cub aside, causing it to fall to the ground. The cub just got right back up to grab the black wolf's tail again. A female wolf with silver hair walked towards Dee as the cub continued to pull at the black wolf's tail. The female looked towards the men and growled, then put her nose on the cub and pushed it around with her head, as if to see whether it was still injured. Then she picked up the cub with her mouth and walked around Dee a few times. Dee reached out and touched the female wolf on its head, and it ran away with the cub in its mouth.

The black wolf held its head up to the sky and howled so loudly that Dee's ears rang. It growled and showed its teeth again and then turned to follow the female. The other wolves started to howl before they too turned away and ran off. When the last two wolves had howled and run off, Solomon went over to Dee and picked her up. He held her tightly in his arms. The guide finally moved. "What just happened here?" the guide asked, "Do we have the photos?" Then he noticed the broken camera and his assistant still frozen. Dee removed the protective shield from the assistant, and he grabbed his rifle pointing it in all directions.

"Calm down, they are gone," said the leader. "I have been studying wolves all my life, and I have never witnessed anything like this. Tell me what just happened."

"You witnessed it, and you are the expert, so you tell me," replied Solomon.

The leader had no response, and Solomon said to Dee, "My heart was racing so fast that I thought I was going to have a heart attack."

"We need to head back to the cage now," said the leader.

Solomon agreed. "We're done for this trip."

The leader and his men started heading back at a fast pace, as Solomon held Dee in his arms and followed.

On the way back, the leader kept shaking his head and looking back at Dee. Then he put the questions to Solomon again without slowing his pace.

"How was your daughter able to calm the wolves? And did you see the light that appeared when she was in the cave? What was that?" Solomon muttered, "You probably saw her flashlight." The leader looked utterly confused, and Solomon refused to say anything more. After the walk and then the drive back to the first campsite, Solomon and Dee ate a small dinner and went to sleep. Before that, her dad said, "I spoke to the guide, and he said you can keep the knife."

Dee heard the leader and his men talking as they sat around the fire. They were puzzling over the events that just occurred. Dee eventually got into her sleeping bag on the cot and closed her eyes. She wanted to leave her body and look for the boy of her dreams. She was intrigued by the wolf's black eyes because they seemed to be the same eyes as the boy. Dee wanted to look into his eyes again to be certain of what she saw.

Dee met the boy at one of their usual places and told him all about the wolves she had encountered. She looked into his eyes and saw that he indeed had the same eyes as the wolf. At that moment, Solomon carefully woke his daughter up because it was morning and time to go.

The Bell Ritual

Dee was six years old and couldn't wait to go on her next wild animal adventure. As they drove away this time, she looked back and waved goodbye to her mom standing in the driveway. Ella stood waving back until one of her other children sought her attention.

After a very long flight, Dee and her father arrived at their destination. Solomon scanned the airport terminal looking for his escorts. He saw two short bald men with orange clothing wrapped around them like monks, and one of them held a sign with Solomon's name written on it. "I'm Solomon," her dad exclaimed, and they greeted each other. One of the monks said he would get the luggage and the other asked that they follow him. At the customs office, Solomon and Dee took a seat outside while the other monk went inside after receiving a folder from her dad.

Meanwhile, Dee had been observing all the Asian people in the airport terminal and the unfamiliar writing everywhere. She knew they were in a foreign country but didn't exactly know where. When the monk returned, he was holding a strip of orange cloth. He held it in both hands and began saying some words in front of Solomon. Then he wrapped the cloth around Solomon's neck and bowed to him. Solomon kept the cloth on as they walked to the car.

The monk told Solomon that they needed to go directly to the ceremony, and afterward, they would be taken to their hotel. The other monk that had carried their luggage waited near a car with the doors open. After driving a while, they came upon an enormous hill with very long steps leading straight up. It was the most steps Dee had ever seen in her life. Solomon took a deep breath and said, "Let's just take our time going up, Little D."

Several monks wearing colorful clothing were carrying incense burners as dark gray smoke billowed over the sides and through small holes. They took <u>large</u> strides up the steps, and Dee began skipping up ahead of her dad. After every seven steps there was a landing, and before she knew it, she had gone up fourteen sets of steps and reached the final landing. There was a sign with symbols on it and sat to wait for her dad. Other monks passed her by, and she noticed that they would all stop and bow to the sign before proceeding.

When Solomon finally reached the top near the sign, he was breathing heavily. He took the herb pouch from around his neck, placed it on the ground and got down on one knee as he tried to pull air into his lungs. Dee put her hand on her dad's left cheek and her other hand on his heart to calm the energy. Solomon took a deep breath and smiled at her. Then he picked up his pouch, deciding that he didn't need anything from it, lifted his daughter up and said, "Thanks, Little D, I feel much better now."

The pair bowed before the sign and walked past it. Solomon and Dee approached an expansive courtyard and saw monks walking towards an entance with tall wide doors. The doors were closed, and everyone waited for them to open. Solomon stopped before they got too close. Soon a rubbing sound could be heard, and the doors to the building started to open slowly, with one door going inward and the other outward. Dee examined the energy around the doors and saw that the right side was more peaceful, so she advised Solomon to go through that door.

Once inside, they saw monks throughout the huge room. A single monk stood on a balcony where he could see everyone in the room. A large bell and a round piece of wood attached to ropes similar to a swing hung above him. The monk would pull the wood hitting the bell once, then step forward and look down at the crowd. He repeated the action until the doors were closed again.

Some people sat on benches against the walls, while others sat on the floor. There were four smaller rooms within the main room, and a monk stood in front of each door. One of those monks approached Solomon and explained what the ritual entailed. Afterwards, they bowed to each other, and the monk returned to his post near the door.

Solomon and Dee sat on a small bench, and he informed her that she would be the third participant in the ritual. Dee saw some of the monks fetching orange material from a big table. Solomon also took one of the orange cloths and wrapped it around his daughter. Then he took her shoes off and told her to focus on what he was going to say.

The monk on the balcony rang the bell once, and Solomon said it was the signal for the first participant to begin. As they watched this person, he explained what Dee was expected to do. "You are to walk to the center of the room where the smaller bell is, stop and bow to all sides. Then you will physically lift the small bell from the table, be very careful not to let it ring. The bell is very sensitive, and the smallest vibration or movement will cause it to ring, so be careful." He also relayed what the monk had told him about the big bell. "If the monk on the balcony rings the big bell during the ritual, the vibration can cause the smaller bell to ring, so you must stay focused on the task."

"What should I do once I pick up the bell?" Dee asked.

"Take it to the table in the corner of the room in front of the old monk and carefully set it down. Then bow, and he will give you a red cloth to tie a bow on the handle of the small bell, and you're done."

Dee had just learned to tie a decent bow on her shoes. "My bow won't be pretty," she said.

"It's okay, Little D. Do the best you can."

She watched the other participants attempt the ritual, and they all failed at the task. When it was her turn, she closed her eyes for a moment and walked to the center of the room. Once she was close by the bell, she looked at it with her second sight to see the energy. Suddenly the monk began to ring the big bell again. He had rung the big bell only once at the beginning to signal the start for the other participants.

Since he was ringing the bell during her turn, Dee immediately put energy around the smaller bell to protect it from the larger bell's vibration. She couldn't help noticing that some of the monks were shocked by the display. The monk continued to ring the big bell, even as she secured the small bell in her hands. Dee completed all the steps of the ritual without the small bell ringing. When she finished tying a bow with the red cloth she received from the old monk. Dee released the energy surrounding the small bell, and the task was over.

Even still, the monk rang the big bell again. She sensed that the vibration just released in the room from the big bell, would clash with the energy she had released from the smaller bell and the people in the room would be affected. Dee pushed her hands out to form a protective shield around her, the old monk, Solomon, and the monk ringing the big bell above. They were the people that she thought would be affected most by the energy clash.

In no time, the force of the vibrations from the big bell came into contact with her lingering energy and created a strong gust of wind. It was so fierce that it blew everyone in the room against the walls. They fought to pull themselves away, but the force of the wind had everyone stuck for a few moments. Solomon and the other two monks had been protected and were not affected by the wind as much as the others, but they all still dropped to their knees and began coughing. Dee was not affected at all.

Once everything was back to normal, the old monk got off the floor and headed towards Solomon and Dee. Solomon put his hands up for the old monk to stop. When he did, Solomon picked Dee up and held her tightly in his arms. "I love you, Little D," he said. The old monk came closer. "Thank you for protecting my people and me," he said. "It was an extraordinary experience, and I have never witnessed anything like it in my life."

All the other monks were recovering, and no one had been severely injured. They all formed a circle in the big room and invited Dee and Solomon into the center. Dee told her dad that she didn't want to join them, so Solomon informed the old monk that they were not going to participate any further and would be leaving. The old monk acknowledged him with a bow, and then invited Solomon to his home to rest. Her dad was older, and not yet ready to take on the steps again, so he accepted the monk's gracious offer. They were escorted to his immense home and shown a room where they would be staying. Dee went right to sleep.

When she woke, Solomon was sitting by her bed watching her. "Dee, you were asleep for two days," he said. "I had to stop them from bringing in their doctors to check on you." Dee sat up in bed, and Solomon gave her some tea. "They made this from the best herbs and berries the country has to offer," he said. Dee smiled and gulped it down.

In the room, there were lots of trays with different fruits and berries on them which the monks had offered to her. Dee looked around the room and saw paintings of flowers and trees all along the walls. The tables and chairs were different than any she'd seen before. They were very low to the ground, almost to the floor. The room was comfortable, large and breezy. Dee drank another cup of tea and ate some of the fruit. "It looks like you're feeling better," Solomon said. "How about you go wash up and then we'll get some sunshine outside?" Dee was pleased with this idea.

When Dee was done freshening up, they walked through the doorway holding hands and entered a colorful garden that was sectioned off into squares. Solomon let go of Dee's hand, and she ran through the garden and trees to play. She stopped running when she saw a small bridge with water flowing under it. Dee walked to the bridge and leaned over to see the water. There were orange and white fish chasing each other in the stream. She turned to look at her dad, as he sat under a canopy with a big smile on his face watching her. She ran and sat with him, and he gave her an apple to eat. He brushed her hair with his hands and told her he would take her to see the Great Polar Bear very soon. First, he needed to rest another day so he could regain his strength for the long trip north. He had been up waiting for Dee to awaken and hadn't gotten much sleep.

Dee was so happy, she jumped off the bench and ran circles around him as she sang, "I'm going to see the Polar Bear, I'm going to see the Polar Bear," over and over again. The old monk came out to see Solomon and seemed surprised to see Dee awake and active. He gave her dad a paper bound with a red bow.

"Thank you," Solomon said, smiling at the monk.

"It is you and your daughter who deserve the thanks," the old monk said benevolently. "Our lives are now joined, and my home is forever open to your family and anyone in your bloodline." He bowed again and turned to walk away.

Solomon and Dee stayed at the old monk's home for two more days while Solomon regained his strength.

Visiting Wild Animals: The Great Polar Bear

After resting at the monk's home for a couple of days, Solomon and Dee prepared to leave. Several of the monks came out to wish them well. So began their long journey north to see the Great Polar Bear. They boarded a private plane and Dee slept until they arrived at their destination.

When the plane landed, a native man came aboard and greeted them. He carried an assortment of heavy winter clothing for Solomon to wear, which included gloves, pants, boots and a coat. He advised that he would have to pick up Dee's winter clothing in town. Solomon carried Dee off the plane and wrapped her up inside his large coat, and she instantly felt warm. Once inside their designated vehicle, the native man drove to a store to buy additional supplies for the trip.

Solomon carried Dee into the store while she was still inside his coat. A lady inside took a look at Dee in her light clothing and began gathering bundles of winter clothes that would fit her. She tried to get Dee to come to her so she could dress her, but Dee stood back. Solomon thanked the lady and informed her that he would assist his daughter.

Dee was kitted out in a snow jumpsuit, shirt, socks, boots, and gloves. Solomon also put a hat and goggles on her head. Then he took a backpack and put another set of clothing inside, filling the pockets of the backpack with a canteen, compass, lighter, light sticks, dried fruit, and some other necessary items. As Solomon put the backpack on Dee, she thought it would be too heavy, but it wasn't. Her father then retrieved another backpack for himself and put an extra set of winter clothes inside, along with items similar to those in Dee's bag.

There weren't any other customers in the store, so Solomon and the native man got into a conversation while Dee walked around looking at the items inside while keeping an eye on her dad. She saw animal skins hanging from the ceilings and stuffed animals everywhere. She made her way back to her dad and asked, "Why does the lady have dead animals and skins in her store?"

"Some people like to keep the animal's carcass and dry and stuff it because it reminds them of when they first saw it," Solomon replied.

Dee paused thoughtfully and asked, "Are there any dried and stuffed people in the store?"

The man chuckled sharply at her innocent question.

"We'll talk about that another time, Little D," her father said with a smile.

"Quite the little girl you have there," the man said, and Solomon nodded.

He advised that they would be staying in his village about thirty miles away, and in the morning they would take the dog sleds and continue to another site.

Dee couldn't wait to see the dogs that ran in the snow. Her dad had told her that they would be riding dog sleds and that the dogs were different than ones she saw at home. They loaded the items they had bought from the store into the vehicle and were on their way.

"How is Mother Metoka?" Solomon asked. "Is she still telling the stories of the ancestors to the children?"

How dad could know anyone in this faraway place, Dee thought.

"Oh, yes," said the man. "Almost every other night the children still sit quietly in her hut listening to her as if they were watching a picture show."

"Great!" Solomon replied. "I want my daughter to hear some of her old stories about the ancestors. Did you remember to get Mother Metoka's sweets and smokes?" he asked.

"Yes, I did," the man replied. "She was delighted to hear that you were visiting again and insisted that you and your daughter stay in her hut."

"Look at the dog sleds, Little D. We're almost in the village," said Solomon.

Dee had almost fallen asleep. She opened her eyes and saw the dog sleds in the village not far away.

There were two big huts, a lot of smaller huts and even a hut for the dogs. The dogs started barking as some men were caring for them while others unloaded the sleds. All the villagers came out to greet the visitors as they were arriving. The escort got out of the vehicle first, and a woman gave him a hug. Solomon climbed out but told Dee to stay in the car. A native woman hugged him as if she knew him, and said something to the people out loud about Solomon but Dee couldn't hear. They all walked over and greeted him, and he smiled and greeted everyone.

An old woman walked through the crowd of villagers. When Solomon saw her, he leaned down and touched his forehead with hers, and they started laughing. Then Solomon turned to open the door and let Dee out. He introduced her to the villagers as his daughter, and people began to approach her. Dee got behind her dad's legs, and Solomon informed the village people that his daughter did not like crowds. They all stepped back and greeted her one at a time, starting with the old lady near Solomon. Dee felt the warm, welcoming energy of the people, and it felt good. She noticed with her second sight that every footprint she made in the snow left a glowing residue of her energy that only she could see.

Once inside Mother Metoka's hut, it was warm and cozy. Four other children around Dee's age, two girls, and two boys were sitting near the fire. Dee stood bundled up near them, and Solomon took off her heavy outer clothing as the children smiled and giggled at her. The two girls began touching her hair as if they'd never seen hair like hers before. Mother Metoka firmly told them to stop.

"It's all right," Solomon said, as he smiled at the children. Dee let the girls touch her hair. Then they all sat watching the fire, as Solomon and Mother Metoka spoke together.

A man came into the hut and told Solomon they were having a welcome feast inside the big family hut for him. The elders were very grateful for the many gifts and supplies Solomon had provided for the village. Mother Metoka reached for the sweets and smokes that the man had given her from Solomon. She smiled and ate one of the sweet candies. Solomon smiled back, then reached into his bag and pulled out a jar of honey. "I didn't forget to bring you some fresh honey from the east. This one is just for you, and there are more jars with the supplies," he said.

Mother Metoka smiled and kissed him on the cheek. "I'm going to make us some tea with the honey you bought for me," she said. She prepared the tea, and they drank it while the women completed preparations for the feast. Solomon then asked Mother Metoka for a favor.

"Anything for you, Sy," she said, smiling affectionately.

"Tell Dee stories about the ancestors."

"That's not a favor," she snorted. "That's what I always do. The children would have it no other way, and even the older ones still come to hear the stories."

Soon the man came back into Mother Metoka's hut to announce that the feast was ready. They all bundled up to go to the big family hut where it was being held. Once inside, the elders thanked Solomon for coming to the village again and for providing so many provisions. Afterwards, Solomon thanked them for letting him and his daughter stay with them and expressed further gratitude for the escorts that would take them to see the Great Polar Bear.

After the feast was over, the people started to sing, and later in the evening, everyone gathered around to hear Mother Metoka tell stories of the ancestors. As she told the stories, the children fell asleep one by one, and their parents took them to their huts. When Dee awoke the next morning, she was in Mother Metoka's hut and saw that her father still sleeping. She was about to wake him, but Mother Metoka told her to let him sleep. She made Dee some tea for them, and as they drank, Dee said that she wanted to hear the rest of her stories when she wasn't so tired and could stay awake. Mother Metoka assured her that she could hear them later since she and her father still had a while before they went home.

A woman came into the hut with some dried fruits for Dee to eat. When she'd finished eating, she freshened up and could hear the children playing outside. She looked at her dad, who was still sleeping, then went outside to play. The children played with the dogs and slid in the snow, having fun together. In the midst of their games, Dee saw that Solomon had woken up and was smiling as he watched her play with the children.

Some men approached Solomon and Dee watched them as they spoke. Her curiosity was interrupted when one of the boys threw a snowball that hit her in the face. All the children started laughing. So Dee picked up some snow and ran after the boy until she caught up to him and smashed snow in his face. This made the children laugh even louder and also caused her dad and the men to laugh.

Suddenly a harsh wind started blowing through the village, cold and bitter. One of the men told the children to go inside. So they all ran into the big hut and huddled near the fireplace to get warm. The mother of the boy Dee had smashed in the face with the snowball came inside and wiped the snow from both her son and Dee. They all began laughing again. The woman then served tea to all the children to warm them up, and it wasn't long before they all drifted off to sleep.

The next time Dee woke up, cold air was hitting her face and it felt like rough paper grazing her skin. She found herself traveling in a dog sled. The dogs were running together as if they were one unit following the lead dog at every turn. She looked up at her dad and slid back under the skins on the sled to keep warm. Behind her dark glasses, all she could see was vast open space. She wasn't worried because Solomon had explained earlier that the dogs and men knew where they were going.

There was a short pause as the lead guide stopped to examine one of the dogs, but soon they were off and running again. The sled had been going for some time when they reached another camp where they saw a large tent. The guide told Solomon they would be setting up camp at the site near the polar bear researchers. One of their guides unleashed the dogs and fed them, while the other began unloading a tent to set up. The first guide went into the researchers' tent. Solomon bundled Dee up in skins, picked her up and followed him inside.

The men in the tent and the villager began talking, and it soon became apparent that they were upset that Solomon had come. They had just lost one of their men when he had got too close to a polar bear. One of the researchers said it was not a good time to see the bears, and warned that his team would not be responsible for anyone's safety. Upon hearing this, Solomon reached into his backpack and pulled out a small black pouch, along with a letter, and gave it to the leader. As his men watched, the man stuck his fingers in the pouch and rooted around but did not remove the contents. Seemingly satisfied, he put the pouch in his pocket and read the letter that accompanied it. He gave the letter back, shook Solomon's hand

and thanked him, but reiterated that he couldn't be responsible for any casualties.

Solomon turned to take Dee's coat off as the man watched in amazement. "It's crazy to bring a young child to this part of the world. This is no place for a child," he said. "Don't concern yourself with my daughter's safety," said Solomon. The man immediately got on his radio and told the researcher at another site to expect the visitors the next day, and that he would not believe who the visitors were.

"What are you talking about, Jim? We've had visitors before," was the reply.

"But not a child," said Jim.

"Put the bottle down, Jim! The only children out here are the polar bear cubs. Call me back when you sober up."

Jim just shrugged and ended the radio communication.

A villager entered and informed Solomon that their tent was ready. Solomon put Dee's coat back on and wrapped her in skins and carried her to the tent where they would sleep, along with the three other villagers. Throughout the night, the village men took turns checking on the dogs, while Solomon and Dee stayed inside the tent, eating dried fruits and nuts. One of the villagers sat next to Solomon. "You should not anger the white men," he said. "They may take it out on us and refuse to trade."

Solomon clasped the man's shoulder and said, "There's no need to worry. I paid them very well, and you shouldn't have any problems with them at all." The man seemed satisfied with the answer and began digging through his backpack. Solomon lay down next to Dee and drifted off to sleep within minutes.

The next morning, they were off again, and as Dee lay under the animal skins, she dreamed of seeing the Great Polar Bear. They stopped to watch a male polar bear they were passing, and Solomon let her look through his binoculars. She saw that the bear was big and strong, and had a red stripe from his face to his stomach. "He probably just killed a seal," her dad said when he noticed Dee watching it.

They continued on their way, finally reaching two old hunting huts where the village men would prepare their animal kills before making their way back to the village. One of the villagers went inside one of the huts and started shoveling snow out, and then took old animal skins that were hanging on the walls and laid them on the floor. He led the dogs inside the hut and they all bunched together lying on the old animal skins surrounding the lead dog. Solomon and Dee went inside the other hut after the men had cleaned the snow out and started a fire. There were so many animal skins inside that it seemed like an animal skin store. They were in four stacks that reached high above Dee's head.

The researcher's tent was over a hill and not far away. They would walk the rest of the way after they'd rested and eaten and had secured the dogs. Soon they headed over the hill. The villager had told Solomon to be extremely careful while they were out because if they came across a bear, it would not hesitate to attack them. "There is a huge mother bear in the area that lost her cub, and the researchers have been watching her for some time," he said. They want to keep out of sight because the bear might attack as soon as she saw them. And with the bear's great sense of smell, she'd know where they were well before they saw her.

The members of the party stayed close together as they made their way up the hill to where the researcher's tent was hidden beneath the snow. There was a hole in the snow that led to his tent. The village men called out to him without going inside, but he did not answer. Dee sensed that someone was approaching and she squeezed her dad's hand, pointing in the direction she'd felt the energy coming from. They stood watching the area for a while trying to see what was there.

Several minutes later, they spotted a figure of a man heading towards them. Dee looked at the man's energy and saw that it was deficient and flowing the wrong way. As he came close, one of the villagers told Solomon that Dee's eyes were very young and special to spot the man as she had. None of his people could see into the vast whiteness like that. The village men looked at each other, then glanced over at Dee, as if they were confused. Solomon told them he would explain later when they returned to the village.

The researcher finally reached them and stood in front of Solomon. Dee moved to stand behind her father as the researcher took off his goggles and looked at her. "I thought Jim had been drinking when he told me a child was coming out here. What manner of insanity is this?" he asked. "It's hard enough for my men to be out here in these dangerous conditions. Why would you bring a child to this place?"

Solomon waited until the man finished ranting before handing him the letter he'd showed the other researcher. He read the letter and handed it back to Solomon. He then looked at the village men and said, "Well, I hope you got paid well enough to bring this old man and young child to this harsh place." The villagers didn't respond.

"Where is the mother bear?" Solomon asked.

"About five clicks to the north on a snow bank near the ocean, hunting for a sea lion," he replied.

Solomon handed the man a small pouch. The man opened it, exposing a precious gem. He held it to the light to examine it. As he did, Solomon said, "I need to borrow the two snowmobiles near your tent."

"You can have them, considering what you just gave me," the man said. "I will even deliver them wherever you want."

Solomon accepted the deal. "Let the villagers keep the two snowmobiles once we're through," he said.

"That's fine, but I will have to return with you, as they are my only means of transportation," was the reply.

Solomon consulted the villagers and asked if anyone knew how to operate the snowmobiles. They looked at each other until one spoke up and said that he did. "Okay then, let's get moving before the mother bear leaves the area," he said. A village man drove one of the snowmobiles with Dee and Solomon on board. Another villager and the researcher used the other snowmobile, while the last villager stayed behind to look after the dogs.

With the snowmobiles, they quickly reached the polar bear. The researcher stopped a good distance away from the animal.

"We can see the mother polar bear just fine from here, and you can even go to the hill to get a better look at her through the binoculars, but be careful," he advised.

"We didn't come all this way to see the bear through binoculars. I could have gone to the zoo if I wanted to do that. We're going to get closer," said Solomon.

"Don't you see how dangerous that is? She can kill at any time, and I won't be responsible," the researcher proclaimed.

Solomon disregarded the researcher and told the two village men they could stay behind if they were worried about the danger. They talked amongst each other, and one of them said.

"My great-grandfather once stood in front of a great polar right before he killed it. The bear fell through the ice, and somehow my great-grandfather secured the bear and returned to the village to get help bringing it back. It took us almost the whole day to get it out of the ice and another day to bring it back to the village. We had enough meat to last the village a very long time, and we had a three-day celebration because of my great grandfather. If I have to die today, then I'd like it to be while pursuing greatness."

"Your courage makes you a great man and your grandfather would be proud of you," said Solomon.

The village men nodded in agreement, and they all agreed to go closer to the Great Mother Polar Bear. Not wanting to stay back by himself, the researcher decided to accompany them and grabbed his rifle. They drove the snowmobiles closer to the bear until the researcher yelled, "Stop! Do not go any further." He got off his snowmobile and took a position behind a snow bank with his rifle in hand.

Dee was so excited that she forgot about the sub zero temperature. All she could focus on was the energy of the polar bear. It was jumping in and out of the water, sniffing the air and shaking its fur each time. Solomon and Dee walked closer to the bear. The two village men stayed close to the snowmobiles, afraid to go any further.

As Solomon and Dee got closer the bear, it growled so loudly that a chunk of snow fell into the water. Dee looked back and saw the village men stepping backward away from the snowmobiles. The researcher was aiming his rifle at the bear, and Dee could feel the fear and tension in the villagers, the researcher, and in Solomon. She tried to ease her father's concern and told him to fix his eyes on her, not the bear. Solomon tried but also kept an eye on the bear.

Dee told her dad to take two steps to the right to block the researcher's rifle's view of the bear. As Solomon complied, the bear stood on her hind legs and growled again. Now within a few feet, Dee turned her attention to the bear and allowed herself to feel the animal's energy. She raised her hands and clapped, then she clapped again, creating an energy field that would protect her dad. That action made the mother bear focus on her, and she got down on all fours.

She moved closer to the bear and Solomon stayed behind. When she was close enough to touch it, the great bear lay down near the edge of the hole in the ice and looked at her. Dee gazed into her eyes for a few moments and reached out to touch the white fur as the bear sniffed her. The little girl ran her hand over the bear's stomach. Then she walked behind the bear and grabbed its fur, trying to pull herself onto its back. The bear used one arm to bring Dee forward. She tried to hug the bear's neck, but her arms were too short. The bear held onto her, then stood up and growled at Solomon and the men. Dee looked at her father and smiled, confirming that she was okay. "Focus, Little D," she heard him say, in a concerned voice.

Then, without warning, the bear turned towards the icy water and jumped in. Solomon tried to reach for Dee before she went under, but it was too late. The next thing Dee saw were pretty shapes made of ice under the water. The bear swam gracefully around and through the underwater ice caverns. Dee wasn't cold and had no problem holding her breath; it felt like she was in a beautiful dream. The bear then went through a big hole and circled around it. The bear let go of her and watched her floating in the water. All of a sudden, Dee saw a big dark shadow pass by. The bear grabbed her close to its chest again and made its way back to the surface.

Once they resurfaced, Dee saw her dad on his knees looking into the water where the bear had jumped in. But they had exited from another hole a little further away. The bear put Dee down in the snow and growled at Solomon. Then it growled at the water before jumping back in. Dee was now freezing and shaking and couldn't stand, so she held out her arms for her father who was rushing towards her. The villager started up the snowmobile and began heading their way. When Solomon reached Dee, he looked into her eyes and said, "I love you, Little D." Dee then realized her dad was running toward the oncoming snowmobile with her in his arms.

She fell unconscious just as Solomon passed the researcher standing with his mouth agape. "She's dead," he said. "No one can survive in the icy water for that long." When Dee woke up, she was at the hunting hut, and her dad had taken off all her clothing and put his coat over her as she lay by the fire. Dee could hear the researcher talking again. "She should be dead. The bear had her under the water for over five minutes; there's no way anyone could survive that." Solomon gave her something hot to drink, and then she passed out again. Her father continued rubbing her skin to keep her warm.

The next time Dee woke up, they were back at the village in Mother Metoka's hut. The children she'd played with before were sitting next to her by the fire, including the boy she'd hit with a snowball. The boy saw her wake up and told Mother Metoka. The old woman got on her knees and smiled at her. Dee could see her beautiful old face and the light of her energy. The woman touched Dee's skin, "You're still cold little one, but don't worry, I'm going to warm you right up." Dee smiled at her.

Then she heard the researcher's voice outside the hut. "She may not wake up," he said. "No one can survive what she went through, and if she does wake up, she will have brain damage. We should go to town to get a doctor."

"I don't want any doctors looking at my daughter," Dee heard her dad say.

Mother Metoka called for Solomon, and he and the researcher hurried inside. They saw Dee awake and playing with the children near the fireplace.

"How's that possible?" the researcher asked. "Do you remember going into the water with the bear, little girl?"

Dee looked at Solomon before answering, and he nodded that it was okay. "Of course I remember," she said. "The Great Mother Polar Bear protected me from the dark shadow in the water and brought me back to the surface."

Dee began to talk about the underwater caves that the bear took her through and the sights that she saw under the water.

The researcher started to back out of the hut in fear and confusion. Solomon told him that one of the village men would take him to town. Then he said, "Remember that the two snowmobiles now belong to the villagers." The researcher was still too stunned to speak and didn't say a word as he left. Solomon spent a little time with Dee talking about her experience, then he went to speak to the elders. When he came back, he saw that she was still playing with the children near the fire.

They all went to the family hut for another celebration, as everyone was talking about the Great Mother Polar Bear and Dee, a story that would be told for generations to come.

Submarine

Dee sat in the living room at home as her dad spoke with someone on the phone. He mentioned the space center, and it piqued her interest. She had visited the NASA space center with her dad before, and it was so much fun that she wanted to go again.

Ella entered the room just as Solomon hung up the phone. "We're going on another trip," he said. "They've asked us to escort a man to the space center and then to a submarine." Dee was thrilled as she and her mom listened. "First, I need to pick up some documents from a judge's estate in Alabama, then drop them off in my safe deposit box," he continued. "Afterwards, we'll accompany the man we are to escort on a helicopter to the space center and then the submarine."

Solomon didn't often tell Ella his plans when he and Dee traveled, and it had been quite some time since they had done any favors. As Solomon was about to say more, Dee noticed her mom unusually paying very close attention to him. She sensed her mom was going to tell someone what her dad was explaining. So, she interrupted him by saying, "Excuse me." Solomon smiled and said, "Go ahead, Little D." But before she could continue, her mom screamed, "Shut up! Your dad is telling me his plans, and I have to remember!"

"There's no need to scream at her that way," said Solomon. "Why do you have to remember my plans anyway?" he asked. "This is not to be discussed with anyone."

"I'm trying to focus like you always tell Dee to focus," she said.

Solomon looked at her strangely and decided not to say anything else about the trip. He asked Dee about her question, and she said, "Never mind." When her dad went to his room, Ella took the opportunity to scold her. "Never interrupt your dad and me again, understand!" Ella demanded. "Yes, Mom," replied Dee. Ella turned in a huff, went outside and slammed the door behind her.

Solomon and Dee left soon after. The first stop they made was the judge's estate in Alabama which they reached in no time. It was a sprawling home with beautiful flowers all around. An elderly black man in a crisp uniform greeted them at the door. He said that the judge was expecting their arrival and would meet with them in his parlor room. Dee sat in a chair until the judge came out to greet Solomon. The judge thanked her dad for coming so quickly and looked down at Dee sitting in the chair.

"Is this the one we've heard so much about?" he asked.

"Yes, this is my daughter," replied Solomon. "Now, let's get down to business."

They followed the judge to an adjoining room where there were all sorts of animal horns decorating the walls. Dee immediately received a physic channel, stopped and squeezed her father's hand. He picked her up and asked what was wrong.

"The animal horns on his wall are from great animals, and there is medicine inside of them that the Shaman could have used to help sick people," she said.

"How do you know this, Little D?" Solomon asked.

"I just know," she said. "The judge should not have such things around him without a useful purpose."

"We'll talk about this later," said her dad, as he sat her down in another chair and proceeded to the judge's desk.

Dee sat staring at the animal horns on the walls. She briefly perceived the agony and rage the animals had felt as their horns were removed while they were still alive. Using her abilities, Dee was able to cope with the feelings coming over her. Then she had a vision of the great rhino. The rhino was trying to protect itself when it was shot. Then she saw the judge through the animal's eyes as he cut the horn while the animal was still breathing and conscious. The animal was in great distress and very angry. Next, she had a vision of a great buck and saw the judge again, cutting off its eight antlers and leaving the rest of the animal behind still living. Dee almost fell out the chair when she had a vision of a great bull elephant as the judge removed its tusk with no regard for the still living animal.

Dee was receiving so many visions and sensing so much pain that she had to block them from coming through. Her dad sensed her difficulty, got on one knee and asked what was wrong. The judge was right behind him.

"The animals spoke to me," she said. "The judge's actions are the reason this is now placed before him."

"What is placed before him?" Solomon asked her, as the judge moved even closer to hear.

"When the judge comes to an end, he is going to a place where there is only pain and suffering," she said. "Only then will he understand the pain he has put upon so many."

Dee took a deep breath and exhaled to release the energy of the animals.

The judge stepped back. "Oh no! Please make her change her view, Mr. Solomon," he pleaded. "I was younger when I did those things. I'm much older and wiser now. I beg you, please, make her change her view of me."

"This has been said, and so it is to be," said Solomon. "There is no change. The ancestors have spoken through her."

The judge looked at Solomon in confusion. Solomon then said, "Now we should conclude our business because time is of the essence."

The judge went back to his desk and slumped down in his chair with a look of distress on his face. Solomon approached his desk without saying a word, and the judge went to his liquor cabinet and quickly drank two shots. He then signed some papers in a manila folder on his desk and gave it to Solomon. Then the judge called for the elderly black man to escort them out. He asked Solomon to please inform him if the child changed her view.

Once in the car, Dee recuperated from the powerful energies that had flowed through her. She laid on the back seat, and her father asked, "Can the judgment be changed for him?"

"Yes, but a sacrifice has to be made," she said.

Solomon nodded. "Don't worry about it, Little D. We need to focus on what's at hand."

Dee took a nap until they arrived at the bank. Solomon carried her inside with him because she was still sleepy. When he asked to go to his safe deposit box, the young assistant bank manager looked him up and down. "Are you sure you have a safe deposit box at this bank?" he inquired with a smirk. Solomon immediately asked to speak with the branch manager, Mr. Franklin. The smile faded from the man's lips, and he turned to fetch Mr. Franklin. When the manager saw Solomon, he greeted him and apologized for his young assistant. He escorted them to Solomon's box. Inside Dee saw lots of gem pouches, documents, and photos of her when they traveled. Solomon placed the judge's signed documents inside his box and locked it.

They headed to a special airport, and when they arrived, they were taken to an office with military security personnel. They weren't in the office long before the phone rang and the security man answered. He kept saying, "Yes, sir," over and over again. Then he advised Solomon, "I was ordered to escort you in my Jeep to the far side of the airfield where a plane is standing by."

Upon arrival, Dee saw a large gray plane with wide arrows on its wings. Two men in suits with automatic rifles deplaned and pointed their weapons at the escort. "I'm just following orders, sir," the escort exclaimed. Solomon showed the men a plastic card and told them to put their guns away. They complied with a "Yes, sir."

The man they were to escort to the space center and then the submarine deplaned. "Let's not waste time," he said. "We shouldn't be in the open." Once in the car, the man greeted Solomon, smiled at Dee and asked, "Is this the child?" Solomon didn't answer. Then one of his security men said, "I was told this was a top priority mission. Why is this child here?"

"Why do you think she is here?" the man replied. "She wants to visit the space center like most children. Now, no more questions about her!"

The security men responded by saying, "Yes, sir!"

Soon they boarded a helicopter and landed at the space center. The man went into an office to speak with someone about a microfiche, while Solomon and Dee waited.

Dee hasn't recovered the full memory of this trip, but she does recall being at the base where Seabees were located. They all boarded a boat that traveled far away from anyone, and suddenly it stopped in the middle of nowhere. Dee sensed that a huge metal tank would emerge from the water. She screamed, "Look out for the big boat coming, Dad!" Several minutes later, a large submarine emerged. "Wow, impressive, young lady, but that's not a boat; it's a very advanced submarine." The man smiled at Dee as he spoke. She wanted to go aboard. "It's not allowed little girl, but you can stand topside," he said. So she and Solomon climbed topside with the man and his two security men.

As soon as she reached the top, she began receiving visions of all the sea life that the submarine encountered deep in the ocean. "This is great!" she exclaimed with delight while looking at her dad. She was overjoyed by the experience. The man they escorted told Solomon, "Make sure you get everything that they promised you for your child, and thanks for your assistance."

Soon other men came topside and saluted the man. As Dee was about to exit the topside, the man they escorted smiled and said, "Remember little girl, it's not a boat." As they floated away from the submarine, the man and his two security men waved at her and saluted Solomon. The captain of the boat said, "I was ordered to escort you to a car that will take you wherever you want to go." Dee fell asleep in the car, and the next time she woke up, they were home.

Ancient Love Story: The 77 Revelation

On November 24, 1972, (77) Dee turned seven years old, and as usual, no one acknowledged her birthday except her father. Since it was her seventh birthday, he thought it was an extraordinary day, and they needed to celebrate. He took her to a shopping area in town in hopes that she would see something she wanted. Dee was always content just being with her dad and happily went along. They arrived at a busy strip mall where people were out shopping for the upcoming holidays.

As they strolled along the busy walkway window shopping, an elderly black man could be seen walking at a rapid pace. He turned abruptly and ran into Solomon, who lost his balance but stopped himself from falling by putting his hand on a store display window. Dee looked up at her father and saw that his eyes had rolled back in his head, and he closed them. The man stood next to him apologizing, but Solomon didn't respond and kept his eyes closed. Dee looked at her dad with her second sight and saw that he was having a vision.

The man waited for him to recover, and when he did, Solomon acknowledged him and said, "I'm okay, no problem." The man walked away but not before apologizing once again.

Her dad looked up and noticed a mannequin displayed in the window of the store wearing a number 77 sports jersey. He paused for a minute while looking at the shirt with a big smile on his face. "I received a revelation Little D," he said still wearing the smile. "Seeing that number 77 shirt confirmed what I now know. Your path is to find the boy you've been dreaming of since you were born. You will know him when you see him because he will have an extraordinary energy similar to mine, but unlike any that you will ever see. His birth date will be July 7th."

Dee was overjoyed. The boy was real! And she could find him someday. "That's what I want for my birthday," she said pointing to the shirt. It was the first time Dee had ever asked for any gift. Solomon smiled as he opened the door to the store. He asked the store clerk for a shirt like the one in the display window in Dee's size. After checking, the clerk informed him that the shirt displayed was the only one they had. Solomon asked if he could purchase the shirt on the mannequin.

"You could, but that shirt would be way too big for her. It's made for a teenage boy," said the clerk.

"That's fine," Solomon said. "I will buy it anyway." He was still smiling as he paid for the shirt and left the store.

"Take good care of that shirt, Little D, and wash it yourself by hand," he said. "That way it will last you a long time, and as you get older, having the shirt will remind you of your path in life."

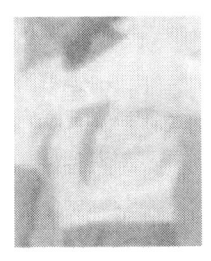

The 77 Shirt

As they were driving home, Solomon saw his daughter smiling broadly, clutching the bag with the 77 shirt to her chest. "You're happy," he said. "Did you have fun walking and going into the store?"

"I'm happy because you told me the boy in my dreams is real and that I can someday find him," she said. "I will know him when I see him with my second sight."

Dee took excellent care of the shirt, and would often sleep in it. The first time she slept in the shirt that same evening, Dee was able to see the 77 boy extra clear in her dreams. She saw him in a forest far away, and they both smiled and ran toward each other. They met in the middle, hugged and began tickling each other while laughing. "Make it rain," the boy said. Dee smiled, and the rain began pouring down on them. They held hands and turned in circles singing, "Rain, rain, make it rain so that we can play in the rain," and the rain came down even more.

Then her half-sibling Emma poked at her, and Dee felt her energy being pulled away from the 77 boy and the dream as Emma darted away. She slouched in her dad's chair upset because she hadn't got the chance to say goodbye before she got woken up. Whenever Dee felt sad when Solomon left her at home, she would put on the oversized 77 shirt and get her blue blanket to cover her face and body. Then she would sit in her dad's chair and dream of the 77 boy, hoping not to get disturbed.

Ella did not approve of Solomon's gift. Although her mom knew of Dee's daily dreams of a boy and was informed about her husband's revelation, she felt that Solomon should not put things into their daughter's head that was "not real," as she would say. Her mom would hide the 77 shirt from Dee in hopes that she would forget about it. However, Dee never forgot about the 77 shirt, it was her most cherished possession.

Once Dee and Solomon spent the whole day looking for the shirt after Ella denied having seen it. Her dad finally found the shirt. It was at the bottom of a stack of folded clothes in her mom's closet. Ella did not dispute the fact that she had hidden it and merely complained that he should not have purchased it for her. During the time the shirt was missing, Dee took a black crayon and wrote "77" on her wooden bedpost to remind her of the boy in her dreams. Although there were crayon marks in her half-sibling's room, Dee was the only child to get scolded by her mom.

Solomon noticed that Dee seemed dispirited and asked her why. "Mom got mad at me for writing '77' on my bedpost," she said. Her dad looked at what she wrote and smiled. He retrieved the ivory-handled knife which Dee got during her trip to see the wild wolves, and began carving a deep "77" into the wood over Dee's crayon marks. Dee was smiling and sat up to watch.

Ella spotted them and entered the room. "Why are you destroying the furniture and putting that 77 mess into her head?" she demanded to know. "I bought all the furniture, which has already been ruined by the other children," Solomon replied. "Besides, Dee's room is the cleanest of them all, and I see nothing wrong with her putting the number 77 on her bed posts."

Ella gave him an angry look. Solomon continued. "If her shirt goes missing again, I'll have to buy her a new one. Should that one get lost or ripped, I will buy more." After that, Dee's mom stopped complaining about the shirt and no longer tried to hide it.

Soon after the 77 revelation, Solomon called in one of his favors and contacted someone to inquire about the 77 boy and his possible whereabouts. When he returned, he told Dee that he had got an anonymous tip that the 77 boy was living somewhere in the Bronx, New York with his mother. Dee was ecstatic, "Are you going to look for him; can I go with you?" she asked. "I don't have an exact address for him and was only told of a particular neighborhood where he may be living," her dad said. "You should stay home this time, and if I find him, I will call you."

Solomon left the next day in search of the 77 boy and Dee waited in anticipation for his return. Solomon wanted the 77 boy to attend the mystery school with Dee so he could keep an eye on her. He searched tirelessly for the boy, even taking to walking the streets and checking local parks and asking people he saw about a boy born on 7/7. After having seen many boys, he returned home a few days later, unsuccessful. That was the last search he made for the 77 boy.

Since they no longer traveled doing favors for influential people, Dee and her dad spent lots of time together. They would visit the cabin, the beach house on Dauphin Island, or one of the other homes to which her dad had access to around the country. Once while they were in one of her dad's homes in another state, Dee saw a maid enter unannounced as her dad was reading. The maid was surprised to see them inside, and said, "Hello, Mr. Solomon. It's been a very long time since you've been back." They engaged in a short conversation before she went to work cleaning.

Solomon sat next to Dee and decided to tell her about U. They hadn't seen U since the ancient cave trip. "U has died Dee," her dad said. "He and his wife were both murdered not long ago," he said sadly. "I know," Dee replied with a smile. "Uncle U called for me when he died, and I went to him." Solomon was outwardly blown away by what Dee had said. He didn't realize she knew of U's demise or of her ability to communicate with him. "Do many people call for you when they die?" he asked.

"Yes, all the time, but most times I don't answer," she replied. "I went to U because I recognized his energy and he was good," she said.

"What happened when you went to U?"

"He was lost in the darkness and was looking for me," Dee said. "When I went to him he was pleased because I showed him the way."

Solomon leaned back on the sofa, took a deep breath and smiled. Then he picked Dee up and squeezed her tightly in his arms. He seemed to be extremely happy, and that made her happy in return, although she really didn't quite understand his sudden mood change.

In the end, we all must go to the dark side. Who could fathom that it all comes down to a little girl?

Epilogue

I am Vince. I was given the task to bring Dee's story to the people and share her light with those who may resonate with it. It has been a very spiritual and eye opening experience for me personally, and I have learned so much. There are messages in Dee's words, and she shares it by revealing the story of her life.

Dee has invested a lot of time handwriting her memories, and I'm so very proud of her. She is, of course, absolutely amazing and I will love her for all of eternity! I hope some of the readers will understand the significance of her story, as well as the offering she has made by releasing her treasured 77 photo. It's truly incredible that she was somehow able to keep the photo hidden, as everything from her past was taken away. The photo was one of the keys to unlocking her stored away memories and starting us on this path of revelation in 2014.

Although both Dee and I lack the tools needed to relay the highest vision of our story, we truly hope that you took some meaning from our words. A lot of time and effort went into writing it, and we would be remiss if we did not express our devotion and commitment to getting the story across in a relatable and understandable way. We hope that you were able to take something out of it and that you saw her story for its beauty and honest truth. Dee went to great lengths making sure her story was presented correctly to the reader and wanted to clearly symbolize a deeper moral and spiritual meaning in the events that took place.

Book 1 focuses on the importance of Dee and Solomon's relationship and the incredible feats she carried out to get invited into the mystery schools. Dee has an amazing ability to use and explore her powers while remaining true to her kind and caring nature. With great power comes much humility, and Dee is a living example of that. She is grateful to have been able to recover her childhood memories and is honored to share them with you.

Dee went on many adventures as a young child. Several of the trips were too short to be added to the book and were not included. She occasionally looks back on her life in amazement at the instant power she possessed, and the good she could have done for so many people in the world. If her life had continued on the path Solomon had planned for her, she would have been quite a symbol for those who may be lost, a living example of an ancient being on the ground with us. But that's a story for another time.

Although Dee earned her invitations into the mystery schools, there were instances when she was approached by others that were interested in her gifts. Solomon took great care to make sure she was protected at all times, but that never stopped strangers from revealing their desires.

There was a time when Dee was seven or eight years old, and she informed Solomon that she needed to stretch. He had no idea what she meant by stretching, so she explained that she needed to go to a large open area where she could run a long distance. Her dad understood and took her to the plains. It was a mostly deserted area of flat grassy land, and Dee very excited to be there.

Once in the open, she ran so fast that it seemed as though she was miles away from her dad in no time. Solomon looked like a small dot to her because she was so far away. It surprised her that she had run so far so fast and she immediately ran back to him. Her dad praised her running ability and said, "Your tiny legs were moving so fast, I thought for sure you would fly." Perhaps she might have flown if given a chance to live her life without being intruded upon.

As Dee and Solomon were preparing to leave, a man with binoculars around his neck approached them. He told Solomon that there were special facilities where he could take his child. He warned Solomon not let his child display her gifts in public. Dee remembers her dad declining the man's invitation to these "special facilities."

On another occasion, Dee recalls a stranger approaching them in a park as they sat together. He was a middle-aged white man in a suit. He advised Solomon that he had spoken to Ella, who had told him where they would be. "Your wife said it was okay to talk to you about your daughter," advised the man. Solomon was visibly upset. He stood up and held Dee's hand, "What do you want?" he asked. The man gave him a card and offered to take Dee away from what was to come. Solomon looked at the card the man gave him and dropped it on the ground. He squeezed Dee's hand, and in an instant, the man was holding his throat and gasping as he struggled to breathe. Dee had temporarily taken his breath away.

Once in the car and driving away, Dee saw the man recovering, as he bent down touching his knees with both hands. During the drive back home her dad reminded her again that "they" would always be watching her. And they continue to watch her to this very day.

Dee's early years were shrouded in adventure, excitement, and danger, but there is so much more.

In Hidden Goddess Revealed Book 2, we continue the journey as our ancient love story replayed in modern times unfolds. Dee is 11 years old, and the boy is 14. She is preparing to visit the first mystery school in 1977, but that plan is made impossible with the murder of her father. Dee is no longer safe or protected in the care of her mom, Ella. The ruling forces continue to manipulate Ella into suppressing Dee, and she endures countless acts of deception and traumatic ritual abuse as a result. Dee is eventually sent to the west and must fight alone against the sinister covert forces trying to stop her rise. It is only through her heart and love for the 77 boy of her dreams that she is able to transcend this dark time. And through spiritual guidance, Dee learns that the boy of her dreams, the 77 Man, is not as far away as believed. And if she can find him, their reunion may very well be the key to her completing her life's journey.

Hiddengoddessrevealed.com

The End

Hidden Goddess Revealed
Book 1
Glossary

Occult: From the Latin word *cultus*, meaning "clandestine, hidden, secretive." Supernatural, mystical, or magical beliefs, practices, or phenomena. The term is sometimes taken to mean knowledge that is "meant only for certain people" or that "must be kept hidden," but for most practicing occultists, it is simply the study of a deeper, spiritual reality that extends beyond pure reason and the physical sciences.

Magick: In the context of Aleister Crowley's *Thelema*, it is a term used to differentiate the occult magick from stage magic and is defined as "the science and art of causing change to occur in conformity with will," including both "mundane" acts of will as well as ritual magic. Crowley wrote that "it is theoretically possible to cause in any object any change of which that object is capable by nature."

Magick/Thelema (2016).

Retrieved from https://en.wikipedia.org/wiki/magick_%28thelma%29

Microchip Implants: Scientists brought to the US from Germany were well-versed in various forms of mind control, and their experiments continued in the US. These programs became part of "black operations," meaning they were not available to the public. Those powers that control the masses have been knee-deep in one particular area over the past sixty years, and that has been to learn how to manipulate and control people. Biblical theology would refer to it as witchcraft, but it is seen as advancement and technological breakthroughs by a government that, on the backside, serves Lucifer, and is preparing the way for his rise and manipulation of the entire planet. Through a combination of mind control and chip implantation, the controlling powers were able to successfully produce the Manchurians.

How to detect and Nullify Chip Implants (2016). Retrieved from http://beforeitsnews.com/power-elite/2014/11/how-to-detect-and-nullify-chip-implants-everyone-has-them-by-now-2447354.html

The Modern Mystery School: The only mystery school that opened its doors to the public on July 7, 1997. The others are closed to the public and are by invitation only. Through the power of activation, initiation, and the wisdom of the lineage of King Solomon, the school provides the tools, teachings, healings, services, classes, and programs that enable initiates to transform themselves, coming into a state of truly knowing themselves.

The Modern Mystery School (2016).

Retrieved from http://www.modernmysteryschoolint.com

The Mystery Schools: A mystery school is a group of initiates who have dedicated themselves to preserving, protecting, and perpetuating the ancient teachings. The initiates are those who are known as the Guardians, the Protectors, the Light Bearers, the Teachers, the Healers, the Record Keepers, the Magicians, and the Watchers, among many other names. There are seven schools, and they are located in North America, England, Romania, Australia, Japan, Tibet, and Africa. Six of them are private and only accept invited students.

Made in the USA
Columbia, SC
21 November 2017